WARRIOR-KING

WARRIOR-KING

THE CASE FOR IMPEACHING GEORGE W. BUSH

JOHN C. BONIFAZ

Plaintiffs' Lead Counsel *John Doe I, et al. v. George W. Bush and Donald H. Rumsfeld*

Foreword by **REP. JOHN CONYERS, JR.**

NATION BOOKS
NEW YORK

WARRIOR-KING: *The Case for Impeaching George W. Bush*

Copyright © 2003 by John C. Bonifaz
Foreword © 2003 John Conyers, Jr.

Published by
Nation Books
An Imprint of Avalon Publishing Group
245 West 17th Street
11th Floor
New York

Nation Books is a co-publishing venture of the Nation Institute and Avalon
Publishing Group Incorporated.

Library of Congress Cataloging-in-Publication Data is available.

ISBN 1-56025-606-0

9 8 7 6 5 4 3 2 1

Printed in the United States of America
Distributed by Publishers Group West

To my parents, for believing that change is possible.

Table of Contents

Foreword by **Rep. John Conyers, Jr.**

This book should be required reading for anyone concerned about protecting our Constitution. In the pages that follow, author John C. Bonifaz describes a critical court challenge brought against the president of the United States on the eve of the Iraq war. The goal: to stop a war that not only was wrong but one that was also in violation of the United States Constitution.

Several weeks before President George W. Bush launched a "preventive war" against Iraq, I received an interesting invitation. Bonifaz, highly regarded as a serious scholar and brilliant litigator, suggested that I file suit against the president to stop the war. I would be joining U.S. soldiers (who were filing as "John Does" to prevent retaliation from the U.S. military), as well as the parents of other soldiers. The lawsuit would challenge the constitutionality of the war on the grounds that the United States Congress had not yet issued a declaration of war or taken any other equivalent action, as the Constitution requires. I readily agreed to serve as a plaintiff. So did Representative Dennis Kucinich of Ohio, one of the most indefatigable congressional opponents of the war. We solicited other members to join us, and, soon, ten others did so.

The lawsuit was particularly timely because other efforts to stop the war, including demonstrations by millions in America and around the globe—unprecedented for a war that had not yet begun—and hundreds of city council resolutions against the war, had failed to avert the looming hostilities.

I was also quick to agree because Bonifaz's constitutional theories matched the arguments that I had made to my congressional colleagues before the House of Representatives passed a resolution last fall purporting to authorize President Bush to attack Iraq. I had voted "no" for several reasons.

First, the Bush administration had not convincingly shown that Iraq was an imminent threat to U.S. security.

Second, it seemed certain that war with Iraq would make us less secure, not more secure, by inciting the recruitment of new Islamic terrorists; by destabilizing the Middle East; by killing thousand of innocent civilians; by miring the United States for years in Iraq, which would have a heavily damaged infrastructure and which would make our soldiers easy targets of postwar violence; by distracting us from fighting al Qaeda; and by expending billions of dollars desperately needed for homeland security. I also noted the conclusion of the Central Intelligence Agency that Saddam Hussein was unlikely to use whatever weapons of mass destruction he did have, or give them to al Qaeda, unless we were about to destroy his regime.

Third, launching a "preventive war" against a country that did not pose an imminent threat to us would set a terrible precedent for other nations. Citing the United States, they might attack countries that they claimed could attack them someday.

The fourth reason was the most fundamental and the one that led to my participation in the lawsuit. In the fall of 2002, I had argued that a war based only on the resolution then before us would be unconstitutional. After countless "Whereas" clauses referencing Iraq, terrorism, weapons of mass destruction, and prior U.N. resolutions, the operative "Resolved" clauses essentially left it up to the president to decide whether or not to attack Iraq. I, like many of my colleagues, argued that, while the Congress was purporting to exercise its constitutional prerogative through that resolution, it was, in fact, ducking that responsibility and passing the buck to the president.

The Congress had unconstitutionally delegated to the president its exclusive power to declare war. In effect, the Congress had told the president: "You decide whether or not to declare war against Iraq." We can now recall how the whole world, not merely Washington, waited for weeks for the president to determine whether we would go to war. (We now know, as we had suspected, that he had decided to do so well before, at least as early as 2002 and probably by late 2001; but that is beside the present point.) President Bush himself summed up this situation when he snarled at a reporter: "I'm the person who gets to decide, not you."

Yet, the Constitution could not be clearer about the power to declare war. It is a power that cannot be delegated.

Our founding fathers wanted the awesome power to take the nation to war to rest solely in the hands of the Congress. They had seen European monarchs, on their personal whims, commit the blood and treasure of their peoples to war. That is why the framers of the Constitution were adamant that the executive would have no role in that decision and confined the president's role to commander in chief once war had been declared. James Madison later observed that this provision was the most important one in that wonderful document.

As the president moved the country and the world closer toward an illegal war, the Constitution had to be defended. Sadly, like the Congress, the judiciary also ignored its constitutional responsibility. It refused to intervene to protect and uphold the Constitution.

In the course of the litigation, many media pundits superficially dismissed its significance. They noted the many hostilities in which the United States has engaged without a formal declaration of war by the Congress.

But, they missed the point. The issue is not one of form. It is a matter of substance. What the Constitution requires is that, one way or another, the Congress must make clear its own decision that America should be at war. That was not done here.

The failure to obtain a ruling on the merits was disappointing and frustrating to all of us involved in that important case. Nevertheless, I remain convinced that it was essential to bring the lawsuit, and I am proud to have participated. It reminded patriotic citizens throughout the country that they can use the Constitution to challenge unlawful government actions. At the same time, it raised people's consciousness about the question of who can commit our country to war. There is no more important public issue. By highlighting and advancing that discussion, in the courtroom and in this book, John C. Bonifaz has rendered a tremendous service to all Americans.

Introduction

George W. Bush is the nation's first president to be selected by the United States Supreme Court. But that's not enough for him. He wants to be king. With the help of the United States Congress and the federal judiciary, he actually succeeded in exercising the powers of a king in the first-strike war against Iraq. If there was ever a time to speak up for the United States Constitution, it is now.

Imagine this: The United States Congress passes a resolution which states: "The President is authorized to levy an income tax on the people of the United States as he determines to be necessary and appropriate in order to pay for subsidies to U.S. oil companies." No amount of legal wrangling could make such a resolution constitutional. Article I, Section 8 of the United States Constitution grants the power to levy taxes solely to the United States Congress. Were such a resolution to emerge, the judiciary would have the duty to intervene to protect and uphold the Constitution.

Now let us turn to reality. In October 2002, the United States Congress passed a resolution which stated: "The President is authorized to use the Armed Forces of the United States as he determines to be necessary and appropriate in order to 1) defend the national security of the United States against the continuing threat posed by Iraq; and 2) enforce all relevant United Nations Security Council resolutions regarding Iraq."[1] Herein lies a tale. Congress cannot transfer to the president its exclusive power to declare war any more than it can transfer its exclusive power to levy taxes. Such a transfer would be illegal. These are non-delegable powers held only by the United States Congress. In drafting the War Powers Clause of Article I, Section 8, the framers of the Constitution set out to create a nation that would be nothing like the model established by European monarchies. This is why they made the momentous decision of whether or not to send this nation into war a matter to be decided solely by the people, through their elected representatives in Congress.

On February 13, 2003, as the nation moved closer to war, a coalition of U.S. soldiers, parents of U.S. soldiers, and members of Congress filed a lawsuit in federal court in Boston challenging President George W. Bush's authority to wage war against Iraq absent a congressional declaration of war or equivalent action. The plaintiffs argued that Congress had unlawfully delegated to the president the power to declare war and, alternatively, that if the October resolution was, in fact, a congressional declaration of war, that declaration was conditional—the use of force being subject to the president's obtaining approval by the United Nations Security Council. Unfortunately, the judiciary stood on the sidelines and refused to intervene.

This book is an accounting of the case we brought against the war in Iraq and the larger implications for our Constitution. Some might ask how George W. Bush's war against Iraq is different from other U.S. wars. Congress has not declared war since World War II. While some of the U.S. military actions since that time have received the equivalent of a congressional declaration, others have not. So from the outset, we are faced with the problem that there have been other violations of the War Powers Clause in the Constitution.

But, today we face an extraordinary moment in United States history. The president of the United States launched a premeditated, first-strike invasion of another country, the likes of which this nation has never before seen. This massive military operation sought to conquer and occupy Iraq for an indefinite period of time. This was not a random act of raw power. It was the first salvo of a new and dangerous U.S. doctrine, a doctrine which advocates the unprovoked invasion and occupation of sovereign nations. This new doctrine threatens to destabilize the world, creating a new world order of chaos and lawlessness. For the sake of humanity, it must be stopped as soon as possible.

Now more than ever, the Constitution and the rule of law must apply. If the president is to put this new doctrine into play, Congress must fulfill its constitutional responsibility under Article I, Section 8 or become irrelevant. The bottom line: If Congress is unwilling to declare war, then the president cannot take this nation into war. And if the president chooses to do so without a congressional declaration, the judiciary must live up to its obligations to uphold the Constitution and to stop the president from unlawfully seizing such power. The very principles of democracy, the very liberty that we claim to export around the world, are under attack. The fate of the nation, and possibly the world, will be determined by our response.

WARRIOR-KING

Chapter One   Elbridge Gerry's Objection

On August 17, 1787, the delegates to the Constitutional Convention turned their attention to war.[2] The question of the day: How would war be declared in the fledgling society, and just who would have the power to decide on matters of war and peace. Pierce Butler, a delegate from South Carolina, sought to grant this power to the president, arguing that he "will have all the requisite qualities, and will not make war but when the Nation will support it."[3] Elbridge Gerry, a delegate from Massachusetts, rose to object. He said he "never expected to hear in a republic a motion to empower the Executive alone to declare war."[4]

Gerry's objection carried the day. The framers knew the dangers of empowering a single individual to decide whether or not to send the nation into war. They had sought to make a clean break from European monarchs, those rulers who could, of their own accord, send their subjects into battle. The framers wisely decided that only the people, through their representatives in Congress, should be entrusted with the power "to loose the military forces of the United States on other nations."[5]

The wars of kings and queens had brought not only havoc and destruction to the lives of those forced into battle and those left to suffer their loss. They also brought poverty. Following King George's War in the 1740s, a citizen of Massachusetts distributed an anonymous pamphlet with this denunciation of those few who had made a fortune from the war: "Poverty and Discontent appear in every Face (except the Countenances of the Rich) and dwell upon every Tongue."[6] The pamphleteer wrote of a few, "fed by 'Lust of Power, Lust of Fame, Lust of Money,' who got rich during the war."[7] "No Wonder," he wrote, "such men can build Ships, Houses, buy Farms, set up their Coaches, Chariots, live very splendidly, purchase Fame, Posts of Honour."[8] They were, he said, "Birds of prey . . . Enemies to all Communities—wherever they live."[9]

Article I, Section 8, Clause 11 of the United States Constitution emerged from this collective memory: "The Congress shall have power . . . To declare war. . . ." No other language in the Constitution is as simple and clear. The framers created only one exception to this exclusive power vested in Congress to initiate military action. An early draft of the language sought to give Congress the power "to make

4

war."[10] Gerry questioned how the country would be defended if suddenly attacked while Congress was not in session.[11] He and James Madison moved to replace the word "make" with "declare."[12] The Constitution thereby reserves "to the president the power, without advance congressional authorization, to 'repel sudden attacks.'"[13] The power to start a war rests solely with the United States Congress.

The framers and the ratifiers of the Constitution shared Thomas Jefferson's desire to create "an effectual check to the Dog of war."[14] George Mason said that he was "for clogging rather than facilitating war."[15] James Wilson, speaking at Pennsylvania's ratifying convention, stated:

> This system will not hurry us into war; it is calculated to guard against it. It will not be in the power of a single man, or a single body of men, to involve us in such distress; for the important power of declaring war is vested in the legislature at large.[16]

Even Alexander Hamilton, the Constitutional Convention's staunchest supporter of executive power would later write:

> The President is to be commander-in-chief of the army and navy of the United States. [This] would amount to nothing more than the supreme command and direction of the military and naval forces, as first general and admiral of the Confederacy; while that of the British king extends to the declaring of war and to the raising and regulating of fleets and armies—all which, by the Constitution under consideration, would appertain to the legislature.[17]

Several years after the adoption of the Constitution, Madison would write:

> In no part of the constitution is more wisdom to be found, than in the clause which confides the question of war or peace to the legislature, and not to the executive department. Beside the objection to such a mixture to heterogeneous powers, the trust and the temptation would be too great for any one man. . . .[18]

In 1848, a young United States representative named Abraham Lincoln wrote a letter to his longtime law partner, William H. Herndon, opposing President James Polk's plans to send the nation into a war with Mexico. Herndon had argued that the United States ought to attack Mexico before it attacked this country. Lincoln's words in reply could not be more relevant for our time:

> Allow the President to invade a neighboring nation whenever he shall deem it necessary to repel an invasion, and you allow him to do so whenever he may choose to say he deems it necessary for such purpose—and you allow him to make war at pleasure. Study to see if you can fix any limit to his power in this respect, after you have given him so much as you propose. If, to-day, he should choose to say he thinks it necessary to invade Canada, to prevent the British from invading us, how could you stop him? You may say to him, "I see no probability of the British monarchy invading us" but he will say to you "be silent; I see it, if you don't."

The provision of the Constitution giving the war-making power to Congress, was dictated, as I understand it, by the following reasons. Kings had always been involving and impoverishing their people in wars, pretending generally, if not always, that the good of the people was the object. This, our Convention understood to be the most oppressive of all Kingly oppressions; and they resolved to so frame the Constitution that no one man should hold the power of bringing this oppression upon us. But your view destroys the whole matter, and places our President where kings have always stood.[19]

More than two centuries after the delegates to the Constitutional Convention drafted and approved the War Powers Clause of the United States Constitution, we are now faced with a president who deployed his lawyers to argue in a federal court that he alone, as the commander in chief, possessed the sole authority to invade another country. Even Elbridge Gerry's old friend Pierce Butler would have disagreed. As it turns out, he voted with all of the other delegates to grant Congress the sole authority to declare war, and he later disowned the view he expressed on that August day in 1787.[20] The framers' intent was clear. This country would never be ruled by autocracy or despotism. No president can hide from this determination.

Chapter Two **The October Resolution**

Just before the 2002 midterm elections, President Bush asked the United States Congress to pass a resolution, one the White House viewed as being politically necessary in the president's march toward war against Iraq. The resolution was eerily similar to the Gulf of Tonkin resolution that Congress passed in 1964 during the Vietnam War. But there were some differences that made the October resolution even more dangerous than that resolution passed four decades ago.

In early August 1964, President Lyndon B. Johnson and Secretary of Defense Robert McNamara announced to the

U.S. public that North Vietnamese torpedo boats had attacked the U.S. destroyer Maddox in the Gulf of Tonkin, off the coast of Vietnam. Secretary McNamara claimed that the Maddox was "on routine patrol in international waters" when it "underwent an unprovoked attack."[21] The story later turned out to be a lie. "[N]o torpedoes were fired at the Maddox, as McNamara [had] said."[22]

> In fact, the CIA had engaged in a secret operation attacking North Vietnamese coastal installations—so if there had been an attack it would not have been "unprovoked." It was not a "routine patrol" because the *Maddox* was on a special electronic spying mission. And it was not in international waters but in Vietnamese territorial waters.[23]

The Johnson administration was desperate for a demonstration of political support for its military action in Vietnam. Two months prior to the alleged Gulf of Tonkin incident, administration officials had met in Honolulu.[24] There, they discussed the need for a congressional resolution.[25] According to the Pentagon Papers released by Daniel Ellsberg years later, Secretary of State Dean Rusk said that "public opinion on our Southeast Asia policy was badly divided in the United States at the moment and that, therefore, the President needed an affirmation of support."[26]

The Gulf of Tonkin resolution stated: "Congress approves and supports the determination of the President as Commander in Chief to take all necessary measures to repel any armed attack against the forces of the United States and to prevent further aggression."[27] The U.S. House of Representatives passed it unanimously. The U.S. Senate passed it 98–2. President Johnson used the resolution to launch a full-scale war on Vietnam, a war that would claim the lives of some 58,000 U.S. soldiers and millions of people in Southeast Asia.

The ghost of the Gulf of Tonkin resolution was everywhere present on Capitol Hill during the congressional debate on President Bush's resolution in October 2002. Like that resolution, the resolution on Iraq did not declare war. Rather, it authorized the president "to use the Armed Forces of the United States as he determines to be necessary and appropriate in order to 1) defend the national security of the United States against the continuing threat posed by Iraq; and 2) enforce all relevant United Nations Security Council resolutions regarding Iraq."[28] But unlike the Gulf of Tonkin resolution, this resolution sought to delegate to the president the power, held exclusively by Congress, to initiate a war. Leaving aside for the moment the sham nature of the Gulf of Tonkin incident, the Johnson administration had at least the semblance of a rationale when it argued the necessity of its resolution. There was, after all, the "fact" of an armed attack on U.S. forces. Here, no such claim existed (despite failed attempts to establish a tie between the September 11 attacks and Iraq). The Bush administration told Congress that the resolution was necessary to preempt some possible future attack, an attack that the administration itself refused to label as being imminent.[29] With that key distinction, the resolution of October 2002 was unprecedented.

There was also another important difference between the Gulf of Tonkin resolution and that of the Bush administration. In October 2002, President Bush was always careful to say that war was not "unavoidable."[30] He said that he had not yet decided to send the nation into war, and he said this as if it were his decision to make. So, why the rush for a debate in Congress and a quick passage of the resolution? Timing is everything. The midterm elections that would decide the majority rule in Congress were only weeks away. As Representative Charles Rangel of New York said during the congressional debate, "We are not talking about a danger like 9-11. We are talking about a potential danger that is somewhere in the future. Whether it is one month or one year, one thing is clear. Nobody has said that we are in danger before November 5."[31] Representative Julia Carson of Indiana put it even more succinctly: "One of the greatest dangers to an American soldier is a poor economy at election time."[32]

The White House cynically pushed for the resolution to be passed on the eve of an election—which means to say that the president pushed for his resolution when Congress was, at best, preoccupied days before a recess and the final weeks of the campaign season. The debate on the resolution was appallingly short, particularly in light of what was at stake. One can only surmise that this was precisely how the president and his closest advisors wanted things to go.

During the debate, Senator Robert C. Byrd of West Virginia, who was unmatched in his eloquence in opposing the resolution, pleaded with his colleagues for more time to debate the matter. Byrd was a senator in 1964 and had voted for the Gulf of Tonkin resolution. Now, he was on the Senate floor to say that, like many other senators from that time, he had lived to regret it. Senator Byrd recounted the death and destruction that resulted from that resolution. He then said:

> After all that carnage, we began to learn that, in voting for the Tonkin Gulf Resolution, we were basing our votes on bad information. We learned that the claims the administration made on the need for the Tonkin Gulf Resolution were simply not true, and history is repeating itself.
>
> We tragically and belatedly learned that we had not taken enough time to consider the resolution. We had not asked the right questions, nor enough questions. We learned that we should have been demanding more evidence from the administration rather than accepting the administration at its word.
>
> But it was too late.[33]

Senator Edward M. Kennedy of Massachusetts rose in support of Senator Byrd. He called for more time as the Senate headed toward closure on the matter after only two days of debate. "Earlier in the session," Senator Kennedy pointed out, "we debated for twenty-one days the Elementary and Secondary Education Act; twenty-three days on the energy bill; nineteen days on trade promotion; eighteen days on the farm bill—all extremely important, but this issue is far more so."[34] "[M]any of the larger municipalities in this country," Byrd said, "would spend a week on an application for a sewer permit. And here we spend two days?"[35]

There were so many unanswered questions. As Senator Barbara Boxer of California said, "I have never seen a situation where the President of the United States asked for the ability to go to war alone and yet has not told the American people what that would mean."[36]

> How many troops would be involved? How many casualties might there be? Would the U.S. have to foot the entire cost of using force against Iraq? If not, which nations are ready to provide financial support? Troop support? What will the cost be to rebuild Iraq? How long would our troops have to stay there? What if our troops become a target for terrorists?[37]

"Today we are being told we have no choice," said Senator Patty Murray of Washington State. "That we have to grant the President war-making authority immediately, without knowing the ultimate goal or the ultimate cost, and without knowing whether we are going it alone."[38]

"Members of Congress should take time out and go home to listen to their constituents," Senator Byrd wrote in a *New York Times* op-ed published during the hurried congressional debate.

> We must not yield to this absurd pressure to act now, twenty-seven days before an election that will determine the entire membership of the House of Representatives and that of a third of the Senate. Congress should take the time to hear the American people, to answer their remaining questions, and to put the frenzy of ballot-box politics behind us before we vote. We should hear them well, because while it is Congress that casts the vote, it is the American people who will pay for a war with the lives of their sons and daughters.[39]

But despite these voices of dissent, most members of Congress, both on the Senate and House side, were too afraid to confront the president on this question so close to an election day. "The President has handcuffed us," Representative Robert Wexler of Florida told the Philadelphia Inquirer. "I'm voting yes on this resolution . . . because I think ultimately the box the President has put us in has forced us to vote in the interest of national security."[40] Senator Byrd put it more bluntly: "[T]he wheels have been greased."[41]

Many of those in Congress who rose to support the resolution premised their support on a central theme: Trust the president. In his floor speech during the debate, Representative Richard Armey of Texas, the then-majority leader of the House, asked: "Should we vote on this resolution that says, in effect that we, the Congress of the United States, the representation of the people of the United States, say: 'Mr. President, we trust you and we rely on you in a dangerous time to be our Commander-in-Chief and to use the resources we place at your disposal'?" "The answer," Armey said, "is yes."[42] Representative Wally Herger of California said: "I firmly believe that our President will make the right decision, in the best interest of the United States, and I have the utmost confidence in the integrity of his counsel."[43]

Yet facts are facts. The framers of the U.S. Constitution created the War Powers Clause precisely to prevent any one individual from being entrusted with the decision to send the nation into war. The framers sought to create a model that differed from those found in Europe, one where decisions regarding war and peace would be made by the people through their representatives in Congress. In October 2002, a majority of senators and representatives ignored that history and, with that, they lost sight of their constitutional responsibilities. In October 2002, the peoples' representatives decided to pass the decision-making authority to the president. In the simplest terms, Congress gave the forty-third president of the United States a blank check for total war.

"The President has solid information," said Senator Kay Bailey Hutchison of Texas, "that with a small amount of highly enriched uranium, Iraq could have a nuclear weapon in less than a year."[44] In other words, pretend we've got a king and trust what the king says. And then, most importantly, give him the power to decide, based on what he knows, whether or not he wants to invade Iraq. This kind of delegation of congressional power, predicated on information held closely by the executive, is the kind of threat to democracy that the framers sought to avoid when they drafted the War Powers Clause.

During his floor speech, Representative William Delahunt of Massachusetts broached a topic that would later come to haunt the Bush administration. He spoke of "disturbing reports" that had recently appeared in the national press "about alleged efforts to tailor intelligence information about Iraqi intentions and capabilities to fill the contours of administration policy."[45] Delahunt introduced into the congressional record two such news articles. One from the *Washington Post* discussed a classified U.S. intelligence report that contradicted Bush administration claims on the alleged threat posed by Iraqi President Saddam Hussein, and called into question the true potential of a chemical or biological attack on American soil or against its interests abroad.[46] The other from the *Miami Herald* cited "a growing number of military officers, intelligence professionals and diplomats [in the U.S. government]" who harbored "deep misgivings about the administration's double-time march toward war."[47] That article quoted one official, speaking on condition of anonymity, as saying: "Analysts at the working level in the intelligence community are feeling very strong pressure from the Pentagon to cook the intelligence books."[48] Delahunt concluded:

> [W]e cannot discharge our constitutional responsibilities by allowing the administration to control the flow of information and simply trusting that they know what they are doing. That is an unacceptable situation in a democracy, Mr. Speaker. And that is not what the founders had in mind when they gave Congress, not the President, the power to declare war.[49]

The memory of the Gulf of Tonkin resolution was repeatedly invoked in the debate. Senator Patrick Leahy of Vermont followed soon after Senator Hutchison's floor speech.

"This resolution," Leahy said, "like others before it, does not declare anything. It tells the President: 'Why don't you decide; we are not going to.' This resolution, when you get through the pages of whereas clauses, is nothing more than a blank check."[50]

"When I came to the Senate," Leahy continued, "there were a lot of Senators, both Republicans and Democrats, who had voted for the Tonkin Gulf Resolution. Every single

Senator who ever discussed it with me said what a mistake it was to write that kind of blank check on the assurance that we would continue to watch what went on. . . . Let us not make that mistake again."[51]

"[T]his nation, that suffered a war in Vietnam, should understand the importance of having the Congress of the United States declare war," said Representative Sheila Jackson-Lee of Texas. [52]

> This system of checks and balances, which is essential to ensuring that no individual or branch of government can wield absolute power, cannot be effective if one individual is impermissibly vested with the sole discretionary authority to carry out what 535 Members of Congress have been duly elected by the people to do. It is through the process of deliberation and debate that the views and concerns of the American people must be addressed within Congress before a decision to launch our country into war is made. The reason that we are a government of the people, for the people and by the people is because there is a plurality of perspectives that are taken into account before the most important decisions facing the country are made. Granting any one individual, even the President of the United States, the unbridled authority to use the Armed Forces of the United States as he determines to be necessary and appropriate is not only unconstitutional, but it is also the height of irresponsibility.[53]

"[U]nlike Iraq," Representative Jackson-Lee continued, "we are a nation that respects the rule of law. And our Constitution, the supreme law of the land, sets forth the duties and responsibilities of Congress in clear, unambiguous language."[54]

"The legacies of wars remain with us forever," said Representative Jim McDermott of Washington State.[55] He should know. From 1968 to 1970, McDermott served in the United States Navy as a psychiatrist. He treated sailors and Marines who suffered from post-traumatic stress disorder resulting from their involvement in the Vietnam War. "I saw firsthand," McDermott said, "the price in grief and anger the troops and their families paid when they were sent into a war whose goals were at best obscure, and at worst deceptive."[56]

"If we pass this resolution," McDermott said, "we are setting precedents that we will regret: that America can start preemptive wars and that Congress can turn over authority to start a war to a President."[57]

The congressman made a prescient suggestion to his colleagues: "Let us adjourn for an hour right now and go down to the Vietnam Memorial before we commit ourselves and our children to an unknown world in which any President can decide to go to war as long as he or she determines it is in the national interest at the moment. Let us look at the names one more time before we wipe away the efforts of sixty years to weave the world together through the U.N. and international law."[58]

More than any other member of Congress, however, it was Senator Byrd who consistently invoked the Constitution and the framers' intent in opposition to the resolution. He rose again and again to object to the resolution. He quoted Madison, Jefferson, Hamilton. He spoke about monarchs of the past and the framers' promise for a different government.

He expressed his exasperation with the limited time allotted to debate a matter of such a crucial significance. He implored his colleagues, over and over, to join him in opposing the resolution.

Byrd's repeated speeches on the Senate floor drew national attention. Tens of thousands of people called and sent letters and emails to his Capitol Hill office. At the age of eighty-five, having spent forty-four of those years in the United States Senate, Byrd became a hero to people across the country who yearned for a leader to stand up against the president's rush toward war.

The senator, known for his command of history, linked the debate to a revolution more than two centuries ago:

Mr. President, here in this pernicious resolution on which the Senate will vote soon, we find the dagger that is being held at the throat of the Senate of the United States. I say to my friends, we ought to pause and wonder if Captain John Parker and his minutemen fought on the green of Lexington for this piece of rag, this so-called resolution. When Parker lost eight or ten of his men with that first shot, is that what they died for, this resolution? Is that what they died for?

How about John Paul Jones, when he was fighting the Serapis. He was the captain of the Bon Homme Richard when he said, "I have not yet begun to fight." What was he fighting for? Was he fighting for this piece of cowardice here in this resolution that gives to the President—lock, stock, and barrel—the authority to use the military forces of this country however he will, whenever he will, and wherever he will, and for as long as he will?

We are handing this over to the President of the United States. When we do that, we can put a sign on the top of this Capitol, and we can say: "Gone home. Gone fishing. Out of business."[59]

The senator continued: "I didn't swear to support and defend the President of the United States when I came here. I pledged on the Bible up there on the desk to support and defend the Constitution of the United States, so help me God."[60]

At another point, Byrd rose to challenge assertions by White House lawyers that the president, as commander in chief, has the power to decide unilaterally whether to send the nation into war:

There is a dangerous agenda, believe me, underlying these broad claims by this White House. The President is hoping to secure power under the Constitution that no President has ever claimed before. . . . I never thought I would see the day in these forty-four years I have been in this body . . . when we would cede this kind of power to any president.

And later on:

[W]e should not shrink from our constitutional duty to decide for ourselves whether launching this nation into war is an appropriate response to the threats facing our people. . . . They are the ones who will have to suffer. It is their sons and daughters whose blood will be spilled.[61]

Referring to the call by some to trust the president, Byrd replied:

They say, "Give the President the benefit of the doubt." Why, how sickening that idea is. Our ultimate duty is not to the President of the United States . . . Our ultimate duty is to the people out there who elected us . . . Our duty is not to rubber-stamp the language of the President's resolution, but to honor the text of the Constitution.[62]

As the debate in the Senate drew to a close on the night of October 10, 2002, Byrd rose to speak for a final time. He quoted Hermann Goering, the founder of the Gestapo, the president of the Reichstag—the Nazi parliament—and a convicted war criminal. In a 1934 speech, Goering said:

Naturally, the common people don't want war but, after all, it is the leaders of a country who determine the policy and it is always a simple matter to drag the people along. Whether it is a democracy or a fascist dictatorship or a parliament or a Communist dictatorship, voice or no voice, the people can always be brought to the bidding of the leaders. That is easy. All you have to do is tell them they are being attacked and denounce the pacifists for a lack of patriotism and exposing the country to danger. It works the same in every country.[63]

Very few senators who supported the resolution, in fact, answered Byrd's repeated constitutional arguments. Instead, their statements on the Senate floor mirrored too closely the strategy outlined by Goering. Many cited the alleged dangers the country faced, the alleged threat of a chemical, biological, or nuclear attack from Iraq. Many also raised the claim of patriotism.

Senator Joseph Biden of Delaware, then-chairman of the Senate Foreign Relations Committee, was one of the few who did address Byrd's eloquent appeal. He said that the resolution was "not an overly broad delegation which would make it per se unconstitutional. . . . "[64] He then claimed, rather magically, that the War Powers Clause in the Constitution allowed Congress "to delegate to the President the power to use force if certain conditions exist."[65] "[T]he authorization we are granting to the President," Biden said, "is tied to defending the national security of the United States in the context of enforcing the relevant U.N. resolutions relating to weapons of mass destruction."[66]

Biden's claim, while wholly incorrect, raised a separate theme that permeated the speeches made by many of those who rose in support of the resolution. While it is true that some members of Congress were fully ready to embrace a unilateral invasion of Iraq, still others asserted that they were voting for the resolution only in so far as they deemed it to be an expedient way to strengthen the president's hand at the United Nations. By demonstrating that the United States was prepared to go it alone, they argued, the United Nations would be more likely to restart an inspection process which, in turn, could help avert war or, at the very least—if such an inspection process were to fail—could help to ensure that any military invasion would be backed by the international community. These voices, it is important to point out, expressed fears of the dangers that would emerge if the United States acted without the support of the United Nations.

Representative Carolyn Maloney of New York spoke of

the assumptions that many of her colleagues in the Congress shared as to how the president would use the resolution once passed.

> We should proceed carefully, step by step and use the United Nations and the international community to disarm Saddam [Hussein]. . . . Just today, I spoke with the British Permanent Representative to the United Nations, Sir Jeremy Greenstock, on this issue. Ambassador Greenstock told me that the members of the Security Council, both permanent and otherwise, will approve a robust inspection resolution; and if this fails to disarm Iraq, he expects a second resolution that may authorize force.[67]

Senator Biden made it clear: If the president could not gain United Nations approval for the military invasion of Iraq, he expected the president to "come back to the American people and tell us what is expected of us."[68] He described an exchange with the president who, at a recent meeting with congressional leadership and committee chairmen, had asked about his position.

> And I said, "Mr. President, I will be with you if you make an earnest effort to go through the United Nations, if you try to do this with our allies and friends. If, in fact, the U.N. does not support our effort, as in Kosovo, and if you are willing to be square with the American people, Mr. President, of what sacrifices we are going to ask of them, particularly the need to have a significant number of American forces in place in Iraq after Saddam Hussein is taken down."

In the presence of all my colleagues at that meeting, he
said: "I will do that." He has never broken his word.[69]

"I am absolutely confident," Biden said, "if it comes time and
we need to go to war, with others or alone, the President will
keep his commitment to make the third most important
speech in his life, to come to the American people and tell
them what is expected of them, what is being asked of
them."[70]

Biden, a leading supporter of the resolution, then followed the example of his colleagues and evoked the memory
of a painful era in United States history.

To do any less would be to repeat the sin of Vietnam. And the
sin of Vietnam, no matter what our view on Vietnam is, is not
whether we went or didn't go. But the sin, in my view, is the
failure of two Presidents to level with the American people of
what the costs would be, what the continued involvement
would require, and what was being asked of them.

We cannot, must not, and, if I have anything to do with
it, we will not do that again.[71]

With the ghosts of Vietnam ever present throughout the
debate, Senator John F. Kerry of Massachusetts commanded a
significant audience when it came time for his floor speech to
announce how he would vote on the resolution. Kerry, a dec-
orated Vietnam War veteran who had opposed the war upon
his return, had yet to make his views on the resolution public.
As a presidential candidate who might challenge Bush in
2004, Kerry was arguably one of the most important backers

of the resolution. Kerry issued his words of caution and his promise.

> In giving the President this authority, I expect him to fulfill the commitments he has made to the American people in recent days—to work with the United Nations Security Council to adopt a new resolution setting out tough and immediate inspection requirements, and to act with our allies at our side if we have to disarm Saddam Hussein by force. If he fails to do so, I will be the first to speak out.
>
> If we do wind up going to war with Iraq, it is imperative that we do so with others in the international community, unless there is showing of a grave, imminent—and I emphasize "imminent"—threat to this country which requires the President to respond in a way that protects our immediate national security needs.[72]

Kerry made clear his conditions for supporting the resolution:

> Let there be no doubt or confusion about where we stand on this. I will support a multilateral effort to disarm him by force, if we ever exhaust those other options, as the President has promised, but I will not support a unilateral U.S. war against Iraq unless that threat is imminent and the multilateral effort has not proven possible under any circumstances.[73]

The senator concluded his speech with yet another invocation of Vietnam.

> One of the lessons I learned from fighting in a very different

war, at a different time, is we need the consent of the American people for our mission to be legitimate and sustainable. I do know what it means, as does Senator Hagel, to fight in a war where that consent is lost, where allies are in short supply, where conditions are hostile, and the mission is ill-defined.

That is why I believe so strongly before one American soldier steps foot on Iraqi soil, the American people must understand completely its urgency. They need to know we put our country in the position of ultimate strength and that we have no options, short of war, to eliminate a threat we could not tolerate.[74]

In the final days leading up to war against Iraq, when it had become abundantly clear that the president would not receive the support of the United Nations, not one of the men and women in Congress who had conditionally voted for the October resolution—with the proviso that any unilateral action would require further justification—stood up to dissent or even to repeat the concerns about a unilateral war. Notably silent were Senators Biden and Kerry whose promises "to speak out" were left unfulfilled.

And what about the central claim—that Senator Hutchison and others believed—that the president had "solid information that with a small amount of highly enriched uranium, Iraq could have a nuclear weapon in less than a year"? The documents supporting that claim turned out to be fakes. Only months later—but still before the launch of the invasion—was it revealed that the allegation of an Iraqi bid to purchase "significant quantities of uranium" from Niger was untrue. On March 7, 2003, Mohamed

ElBaradei, the director-general of the International Atomic Energy Agency in Vienna reported to the U.N. Security Council on the documents in the alleged Niger-Iraq uranium sale: "The I.A.E.A. has concluded, with the concurrence of outside experts, that these documents . . . are, in fact, not authentic."[75] A senior I.A.E.A. official told Seymour M. Hersh of *The New Yorker* that the fabrications were so obvious that "they could be spotted by someone using Google on the Internet."[76] On March 14, 2003, less than a week before the invasion of Iraq was under way, Senator Jay Rockefeller of West Virginia, the senior Democrat on the Senate Intelligence Committee sent a letter to Robert Mueller, the FBI Director, formally requesting an investigation of the forged documents. Rockefeller, who—unlike West Virginia's other senator—voted for the resolution, wrote: "There is a possibility that the fabrication of these documents may be part of a larger deception campaign aimed at manipulating public opinion and foreign policy regarding Iraq."[77]

The revelation of the forged documents just days prior to the launch of an invasion of Iraq only underscored the need for judicial intervention. The alleged Iraqi nuclear threat had served as a critical basis for the passage of the October resolution. Now, like the Gulf of Tonkin resolution, there were signs that the congressional vote in October may have been premised on falsehoods. The ghost of that Vietnam-Era resolution was still in the house.

With the Constitution in the balance, the judiciary would face an opportunity to ensure that the mandate of the War Powers Clause be followed: that no one individual—not even the president of the United States—can be entrusted with the decision to send the nation into war. For the first one hundred and fifty years of the nation's history, the judiciary had essentially fulfilled this responsibility. Then, following World War II, the erosion of the constitutional mandate, accompanied by judicial inaction, began. As dangerous as that erosion had been, President Bush's march toward a preemptive first-strike war had no match. A challenge to the president's authority to launch such an invasion of another country would mark a defining moment for the judiciary and for the Constitution.

Chapter Three **War in the Courtroom**

United States soldiers do not ordinarily file lawsuits against a president of the United States. When they do, it is worth taking notice.

In February 2003, three U.S. soldiers stepped forward to lead a coalition challenging President Bush's authority to wage war against Iraq absent a congressional declaration of war. The soldiers included a United States Marine based in the Persian Gulf. Joined by members of Congress and parents of soldiers from around the country, they sued the president and Secretary of Defense Donald H. Rumsfeld seeking to prevent the launch of a military invasion of Iraq without

Congress either first declaring war or taking equivalent action.

U.S. soldiers had brought cases during the Vietnam War challenging the constitutionality of that war. Yet, those cases were filed when there was still a military draft in this country. Today, we have a volunteer army. When people enlist today to join the U.S. Armed Forces, they do so accepting that they must obey the rules. They do so knowing that, one day, they might be called upon to fight and die for their country.

The rules also apply to the president, as commander in chief. The rules prevent the president from sending U.S. soldiers into battle in an offensive war unless the president first seeks and receives a declaration of war or equivalent action from the United States Congress. The soldiers, whose identities were protected in the case, argued that they were ready to follow the rules but that they should not be forced to fight an illegal and unconstitutional war.

The presence of these soldiers in this lawsuit was crucial for two reasons. First, it revealed dissent within the military ranks on whether the president had the constitutional authority to wage war. The president's supporters might try to question the motives of Democratic members of Congress who challenged his authority. They could not question the motives of these soldiers. For what exactly were they being asked to fight and possibly die for if the war was in direct violation of the U.S. Constitution?

From a legal perspective, with soldiers as plaintiffs in the case, the president's lawyers could not get the complaint dismissed on standing grounds. The parents of soldiers and the members of Congress had tougher arguments for why they had standing to bring this constitutional claim. (Standing is a requirement for a court to hear a case; plaintiffs have standing if they are directly harmed by the actions of the defendents and if the court has the ability to remedy that harm.) In prior war powers cases, some courts had refused to review the actual claims, ruling instead that the plaintiffs were not the proper parties to bring such cases. The courts have also ruled, however, that so long as one party has standing, it is not necessary that the other parties meet the standing test. The soldiers in this case could argue forcefully, more than any other plaintiff who had signed on to the case, that they had the right to be heard on the merits of their claim. After all, they were the ones who would be sent to fight in this war. They deserved to have their claim—that this war was illegal—addressed by the courts.

On the morning of February 13, 2003, we filed our case, *John Doe I v. President Bush* in federal district court in Boston. We held a press conference in the Old South Meeting House in the downtown section of the city. It was a fitting venue. On December 16, 1773, more than 5,000 colonists had crowded into the Old South Meeting House to debate a controversial tea tax. The meeting sparked the Boston Tea Party, the celebrated protest against the British monarchy in which the colonists dumped 342 chests of tea into the Boston Harbor.

Two hundred and thirty years later, Charley Richardson, the father of a U.S. Marine based in the Persian Gulf, stood before a bank of microphones and television cameras. Richardson was there to explain why he was among the plaintiffs filing suit that day against the president.

"As the father of a United States Marine," Richardson said, "there is only one thing worse than the prospect of receiving a call telling me that my son Joe has been killed in battle. It is the prospect of being told that he has been killed fighting an illegal and unconstitutional war."

Nancy Lessin, Richardson's wife and the stepmother of Joe, was there as well. She held a photo of Joe for the cameras. "We notice," she said, "that those who say 'we gotta go to war' aren't going anywhere—nor are their loved ones. It is other people's children who are now in harm's way—our children." She said a momentous decision to send the nation into war could not be made by one person. Such a decision had to be made by the U.S. Congress.

Their eloquent voices matched the spirit of the building in which they stood. Like those before them, theirs was a challenge to the abuse of power—and a demand that other voices be heard.

With the identities of the soldier-plaintiffs protected from the public, Nancy Lessin and Charley Richardson became the most visible plaintiffs in the case, providing a powerful human face to the legal claims. In November 2002, they had co-founded, with another parent-plaintiff Jeffrey MacKenzie, Military Families Speak Out, an advocacy group for people whose loved ones were in the military and who were opposed to a war against Iraq. They had stood up before, opposing the war in Vietnam. They were standing up again, ready to go anywhere, speak anywhere. The march to another war, without the consent of the people of the country, felt all too familiar.

Reporters gathered at the Old South Meeting House that

morning to ask a series of questions that would be repeated throughout the litigation process. Congress has not declared war since World War II; why is this situation any different than prior U.S. wars since that time? What about the resolution passed by Congress in October 2002? Didn't that authorize the president to launch a war? Don't the soldiers in the case have to obey the commander in chief? How do they have the right to sue him?

At the heart of these questions is the fundamental issue of the role of the judiciary in matters of war and peace. Many of those gathered seemed to accept the assumption that the president could, in effect, declare war against any country of his choosing. Only weeks before, a reporter had opined to the president that a war against Iraq was inevitable. The president had angrily responded: "I'm the person who gets to decide, not you."[78] In this climate, regardless of the rule of law and the Constitution, the supposition that our courts could play a role in reviewing such a momentous issue actually represented a challenge to conventional thinking.

"It is emphatically the province and the duty of the judicial department to say what the law is."[79] Chief Justice John Marshall wrote those words in 1803 for a unanimous United States Supreme Court in the landmark case of *Marbury v. Madison*. For the first time in the nation's young history, the ruling established the principle of judicial review. Courts have the responsibility and the power to review the actions of the legislative and executive branches and to ensure that they are consistent with the United States Constitution. The exercise of this power by the judiciary has helped to maintain the Constitution as a living, breathing document for more than two centuries. If a president, therefore, demonstrates his intent to violate the Constitution, the courts have a duty to act.

When it comes to matters dealing with the War Powers Clause of the Constitution, the Supreme Court has a long history of intervening to prevent a president from engaging in the unlawful seizure of power. In 1804, as hostilities grew with France, the Court held that the president could not authorize the taking of a ship sailing *from* a French port, as Congress had only authorized the capture of ships sailing to a French port.[80] In 1814, the Court held that neither Congress's declaration of war launching the War of 1812 nor any other statute gave the executive branch the authority to take enemy property located within the United States.[81] In 1850, the court held that the president did not have the authority to seize territory by virtue of military conquest in the Mexican War.[82] Other cases from that first century of *Marbury*'s mandate demonstrated the judiciary's willingness to review the constitutionality of the executive branch's conduct in war.

Such court precedent is critical in the litigation of any case. In making legal arguments before a court, lawyers will often cite prior rulings on similar issues. This is not to say that courts will follow precedent every time; it is to say that a strong case can be built on such precedent.

Yet we need not go back to the nineteenth century to find a Supreme Court fulfilling its judicial review responsibility in a war powers case. The most recent example can be found in the Court's 1952 ruling in *Youngstown Sheet & Tube Co. v. Sawyer,* still the most influential Supreme Court decision regarding executive power.[83]

In 1952, in the midst of growing public opposition to the Korean War, President Harry Truman faced an announced nationwide strike of steelworkers arising from a labor dispute between steel companies and their employees.[84] Hours before the strike was to begin, Truman responded by issuing Executive Order 10340, "directing the Secretary of Commerce to take possession of and operate the plants and facilities of eighty-seven major steel companies."[85] The order cited the Korean War as justification for this action and called steel "'indispensable' for producing weapons and war materials.'"[86]

Following the issuance of this executive order, the secretary of commerce, Charles Sawyer, immediately directed "the presidents of the various seized companies to serve as operating managers for the United States."[87] Truman sent a message to Congress the day after issuing the order, reporting his action. He sent a second message twelve days later. Congress remained silent.[88]

The steel companies, while obeying the order under protest, filed suit against the commerce secretary in federal district court in Washington, charging that the seizure lacked any constitutional or statutory basis, and they sought an injunction to prevent the continued enforcement of the action.[89] The U.S. Justice Department, representing Sawyer, argued in court that Truman had inherent executive power to issue the order, "power 'supported by the Constitution, by historical precedent, and by court decisions.'"[90] Assistant Attorney General Homer Baldridge told U.S. District Court Judge David A. Pine "that courts were powerless to control the exercise of presidential power when directed toward emergency conditions."[91] A reporter asked Truman at a press conference, "if he could seize the steel mills under his inherent powers, could he 'also seize the newspapers and/or radio stations?'"[92] Truman replied: "Under similar circumstances the president of the United States has to act for whatever is best for the country."[93]

Judge Pine firmly rejected this claim of inherent executive power. He issued a preliminary injunction restraining the commerce secretary from continuing the seizure of the steel mills. While recognizing the extensive harm a nationwide steel strike could inflict on the country, Judge Pine wrote that a strike "would be less injurious to the public than the injury which would flow from a timorous judicial recognition that there is some basis for this claim to unlimited and unrestrained Executive power, which would be implicit in a failure to grant the injunction."[94]

The Supreme Court agreed to hear the case on a rare expedited schedule and, within weeks, issued a 6–3 ruling affirming Judge Pine's decision. The Court stated:

> The order cannot properly be sustained as an exercise of the President's military power as Commander in Chief of the Armed Forces. . . . Even though "theater of war" be an expanding concept, we cannot with faithfulness to our constitutional system hold that the Commander in Chief of the Armed Forces has the ultimate power as such to take possession of private property in order to keep labor disputes from stopping production. This is a job for the Nation's lawmakers, not for its military authorities.[95]

Justice William O. Douglas, in his concurring opinion, addressed the president's claims of an emergency giving rise to the issuance of his executive order.

> All executive power—from the reign of ancient kings to the rule of modern dictators—has the outward appearance of efficiency. Legislative power, by contrast is slower to exercise. . . . We therefore cannot decide this case by determining which branch of government can deal most expeditiously with the present crisis. The answer must depend on the allocation of powers under the Constitution.[96]

"If we sanctioned the present exercise of power by the President," he continued, "we would be expanding Article II of the Constitution and rewriting it to suit the political conveniences of the present emergency."[97] Justice Douglas concluded:

> We pay a price for our system of checks and balances, for the distribution of power among the three branches of government. It is a price that today may seem exorbitant to many. Today a kindly President uses the seizure power to effect a wage increase and to keep the steel furnaces in production. Yet tomorrow another President might use the same power to prevent a wage increase, to curb the trade unionists, to regiment labor as oppressively as industry thinks it has been regimented by this seizure.[98]

Justice Robert H. Jackson was as equally eloquent in his concurring opinion: "With all its defects, delays and inconveniences," he wrote, "men have discovered no technique for long preserving free government except that the Executive be under the law, and that the law be made by parliamentary deliberations. Such institutions may be destined to pass away. But it is the duty of the Court to be last, not first, to give them up."[99]

Faced with a president claiming inherent executive power during a time of war and a Congress acquiescing to that power through its silence, the judiciary in Youngstown intervened and protected the Constitution. Like many prior war powers cases in the nation's history, the Supreme Court responded to the *Marbury v. Madison* mandate and rightly exercised its power to act.

The Korean War also opened a new era in this country's jurisprudence on the question of war and peace. While earlier war powers cases addressed actions taken by the executive branch during wartime, "until Korea, few occasions arose for direct judicial inquiry into the legality of an American war."[100] Prior to the Korean War, "no president had committed American troops to prolonged combat without meticulously complying with the letter of Article I, Section 8, clause 11 of the Constitution."[101]

President Truman broke that pattern. In June 1950, in response to the invasion of South Korea by the North Korean army, Truman ordered "United States air and sea forces to give the [South] Korean Government troops cover and support."[102] The action marked the beginning of U.S. involvement in the Korean War. Truman never sought approval from Congress for the U.S. participation in this war and "Congress's reaction to Truman's usurpation of war power was largely passive."[103] Truman's secretary of state Dean Acheson stated that, when it came to consulting with Congress about the war, the president might "tell them what had been decided."[104] It was a terrible blow to the Constitution. Congress never issued a declaration of war.

In 1951, the federal judiciary had an opportunity to intervene. James M. Bolton, who had received a notice from his local draft board, refused to report for induction into the U.S. Armed Forces. The federal government charged Bolton with violating the Selective Service Act of 1948. In his defense, Bolton argued that the act was unconstitutional since, as applied, it drafted men to fight in the Korean War "without any declaration of war by Congress and 'without the consent of Congress.'"[105] A federal district court judge convicted Bolton and sentenced him to a year in prison. Bolton appealed the conviction, raising again his constitutional claim before the federal appeals court. The appeals court affirmed the judge's ruling, finding that Bolton did not have standing to make his claim since his order to report for induction did not amount to an order to fight in the Korean War. The court stated: "Any question as to the legality of an order sending men to Korea to fight in an 'undeclared war' should be raised by someone to whom such an order has been directed, not by the appellant, who might never be ordered abroad for military duty, even if he reported for induction."[106]

The standing barrier appeared again in the early court challenges to the Vietnam War.[107] In December 1964, David Mitchell, a leader of the draft resistance movement during that war, received an order from his local draft board to report for induction in the U.S. Armed Forces. Mitchell refused to comply. Like Bolton, Mitchell argued that he should not be forced to fight in a war "undeclared by Congress and in effect declared by the executive."[108] A federal district court convicted Mitchell of violating the Universal Military Training and Service Act and sentenced him to a minimum of eighteen months in prison. The court found that Mitchell "lack[ed] standing to claim that the Act is being unconstitutionally applied in drafting him to go to Vietnam to fight an 'undeclared war.'"[109] "Had he been inducted," the court continued, "he might never have been sent abroad, much less to Vietnam. Until inducted and ordered to Vietnam, his claim of unconstitutional application of the Act is premature."[110]

While finding that Mitchell did not have standing to make his constitutional argument, the district court, nevertheless, sought to refute the claim in one page of its ruling. The court acknowledged that Congress had "not formally declared war with respect to military action in Vietnam," but stated that it had "given its wholehearted approval to the action of the President by appropriations and other implementing legislation."[111] Mirroring the basis for the Gulf of Tonkin resolution, the court also argued that the president has the power to "start the gun at home or abroad to meet force with force" and that "this power must extend to repelling attacks upon our allies which threaten our security."[112]

The district court did little to hide its contempt for Mitchell's views. Mitchell had stated, in support of his motion to dismiss the indictment, that he "must disassociate himself from the war crimes of his government" with respect to the Vietnam War.[113] In revealing language, the court referred to "the sickening spectacle of a twenty-two-year old citizen of the United States seizing the sanctuary of a nation dedicated to freedom of speech to assert such tommyrot."[114]

A federal appeals court upheld Mitchell's conviction, though on narrower grounds. It found only that Mitchell could not make his claims as a defense to a prosecution for failure to report for induction, arguing that, regardless of "[w]hatever action the President may order," Congress has the power—as exercised through the Act—"'to raise and support armies' and 'to provide and maintain a navy.' . . . ."[115]

As the United States deepened its involvement in Vietnam and the legal challenges continued, the courts shifted from relying principally on the standing barrier and began to invoke the doctrine of "political question" to bar consideration of the merits of any constitutional claims. The political question doctrine is cited with respect to matters that a court believes should be resolved only by the political branches of government. While it is legitimately applied in some cases, courts too often invoke the doctrine as a means of avoiding the constitutional responsibility of judicial review.

In fact, two years prior to the Gulf of Tonkin resolution, the Supreme Court, in the landmark ruling of *Baker v. Carr,* made it clear that the political question doctrine had no place in a constitutional challenge to malapportioned legislative districts in Tennessee.[116] Lower courts had refused to reach the merits of the plaintiffs' claims that Tennessee's 1901 apportionment statute, by which the state allocated legislative representation among its counties, debased their votes and thereby violated the Equal Protection Clause of the Fourteenth Amendment to the U.S. Constitution. The courts had ruled that the plaintiffs' complaint belonged in the Tennessee legislature, not in the judiciary. In fact, the Tennessee Supreme Court, in deciding the state court case that preceded the federal court challenge, warned of the gravest of dangers if the judiciary were to intervene in the apportionment issue: "The ultimate result of holding this Act unconstitutional . . . would be to deprive us of the present Legislature and the means of electing a new one and ultimately bring about the destruction of the State itself."[117]

The U.S. Supreme Court rejected the argument that the case presented a political question unfit for judicial review. "The right asserted is within the reach of judicial protection under the Fourteenth Amendment."[118] The Baker ruling initiated the series of historic "one person, one vote" cases which resulted in reapportioned legislatures throughout the country. Two years following that ruling, in a case dealing with the apportionment of seats in the Alabama legislature, the Supreme Court addressed directly the warnings against judicial intervention in the matter:

> We are told that the matter of apportioning representation in a state legislature is a complex and many-faceted one. We are advised that States can rationally consider factors other than population in apportioning legislative representation. We are admonished not to restrict the power of the States to impose differing views as to political philosophy on their citizens. We are cautioned about the dangers of entering into political thickets and mathematical quagmires. Our answer is this: a denial of constitutionally protected rights demands judicial protection; our oath and our office require no less of us.[119]

The Supreme Court, however, did not apply this same resolve with respect to constitutional challenges to the Vietnam War. Instead, when it came to claims that the United States was engaged in an illegal and unconstitutional war in Vietnam—with the lives of millions of people at stake—the Court repeatedly chose to stand on the sidelines.

Robert Luftig's case represents one of the first in which the courts invoked the political question doctrine to avoid reviewing a constitutional challenge to the Vietnam War. Luftig was a private in the United States Army who filed suit in 1966 in federal court in Washington against Secretary of Defense Robert McNamara and Secretary of the Army Stanley Resor. He argued that the war in Vietnam was unconstitutional and that the defendants had no lawful authority to send him there.[120] Unlike David Mitchell, however, Luftig was not a draft resistance leader. He did not challenge the legality of his induction nor did he seek release from military duty.[121]

The federal appeals court in Washington affirmed a federal district court judge's dismissal of the case on political question grounds. It stated that "resort to the courts is futile, in addition to being wasteful of judicial time, for which there are urgent legitimate demands."[122] "The fundamental division of authority and power established by the Constitution," the court continued, "precludes judges from overseeing the conduct of foreign policy or the use and disposition of military power; these matters are plainly the exclusive province of Congress and the Executive."[123] In essence, the court asserted that the claim of a presidential violation of the War Powers Clause could never be reviewed by the judicial branch.

Alongside Luftig's case came the case of David Mora,

James Johnson, and David Samas, who also brought suit in Washington against McNamara and Resor. These three men had been drafted into the United States Army in late 1965. They had all received orders to fight in Vietnam.[124] And like Luftig, their claims regarding the illegality of the war were blocked from judicial review on political question grounds.

The Supreme Court refused to hear either case. Yet in the *Mora* case, two Supreme Court justices issued rare dissenting opinions to the Court's denial of a petition for review. Justice Potter Stewart joined Justice Douglas who had previously dissented in the Court's refusal to take the *Mitchell* case for review. Justice Stewart identified several questions "of great magnitude" raised in the case.[125] Included in that list were the questions of whether the U.S. military action in Vietnam constituted "a 'war' within the meaning of Article I, Section 8, Clause 11, of the Constitution" and whether, if it did, the executive branch was in the position to "constitutionally order the petitioners to participate in that military activity, when no war has been declared by the Congress."[126] "These are large and deeply troubling questions. . . . " Stewart wrote, "[w]e cannot make these problems go away simply by refusing to hear the case of three obscure Army privates."[127]

> [A]s Justice Stewart's dissenting opinion revealed, the legal issues raised by the war in Vietnam had nothing whatever to do with the wisdom or propriety of the war, but rather focused solely upon whether the president could wage a major war in Vietnam without the authorization of Congress—a classical judicial question, calling for the traditional process of constitutional interpretation. . . . [A] soldier with

orders to go to Vietnam could complain both that the Constitution was being violated and that the violation endan-
gered his life. The federal courts were instituted to hear
precisely those kinds of complaints. If they did not, who
would?[128]

As Justice Douglas stated in yet another dissenting opinion
issued a year later to a Supreme Court denial of a petition to
review this constitutional claim: "I think we owe to those who
are being marched off to jail for maintaining that a declaration of war is essential for conscription an answer to this
important constitutional question."[129]

The federal judiciary's refusal to review the merits of a
constitutional challenge to the Vietnam War continued until
the summer of 1970 when Malcolm Berk and Salvatore
Orlando initiated their cases. As Leon Friedman and Burt
Neuborne, two of the lead attorneys for Berk and Orlando,
write in their book, *Unquestioning Obedience to the President:
The ACLU Case Against the Legality of the War in Vietnam,*
"Two events of considerable import preceded and undoubt-
edly influenced the Berk and Orlando breakthroughs."[130]

First, Friedman and Neuborne point out, in April 1970,
growing opposition to the war led the Massachusetts legislature to pass a statute "directing the state attorney general to
challenge the war's legality on behalf of Massachusetts resi-
dents ordered to Vietnam."[131] The passage of the law "set the
stage for a new and intensive researched attempt to secure
judicial review of the war."[132]

The following month, in May 1970, President Richard
Nixon and Secretary of State Henry Kissinger "launched an

invasion of Cambodia, after a long bombardment that the government never disclosed to the public."[133] Friedman and Neuborne write that "[t]he dangers of untrammeled presidential power in the area of war and peace were acutely revealed by Cambodia, and the prospects for judicial review of presidential warmaking increased accordingly."[134]

That same year, Theodore C. Sorensen, a former key aide to President John F. Kennedy, was running for the Democratic nomination for United States Senate from New York. In researching whether New York should follow the lead of Massachusetts and pass a similar statute to create another court challenge to the war, Sorensen's campaign discovered a 1787 New York law which "forbid the shipment of New York soldiers out of state, except in cases specifically provided for in the federal Constitution."[135] The campaign issued a press release highlighting the long-forgotten law.[136] Soldiers flooded Sorensen's campaign with phone calls seeking legal representation to challenge their orders to be sent to Vietnam.[137] Malcolm Berk was one of them.

Berk's case marked the first challenge to the Vietnam War in which a court reviewed the underlying constitutional claims. At oral argument before U.S. District Court Judge Orrin G. Judd, Sorensen, representing Berk, refuted the claim that the case was barred by the political question doctrine: "To say that this is a political issue—that it is not a justiciable case—is to say that there is no such thing as an unconstitutional war; that there is no restraint on the exercise of the powers of the president who wishes to send American forces in combat anywhere in the world."[138] At the close of that court argument on June 5, 1970, Judge Judd denied Berk's request for a preliminary injunction, stating that, even if it were established that the court had the right to review the case, Berk was not likely to succeed on the merits of his claims. Faced with an order to be sent to Vietnam two days later, Berk, through his attorneys, sought a temporary stay of the order, which would allow for the appeal of his case to the federal appeals court.[139] A federal appeals court judge refused to issue the stay, but on further appeal, Supreme Court Justice Byron White granted the request, "ordering that Berk temporarily remain within the country."[140]

Justice White's stay order led to the filing of new challenges to the war, including one brought by Salvatore Orlando.[141] Orlando had enlisted twice in the United States Army and, in June 1970, he had received an order to be sent to Vietnam. Days after Justice White's order, Orlando filed his case in federal district court in New York.

Before the district court heard Orlando's motion for a preliminary injunction, the U.S. Court of Appeals for the Second Circuit issued its first ruling in the *Berk* case. The appeals court did something remarkable. For the first time, a court opened the door for consideration of the merits of this constitutional claim against an undeclared war. The court remanded the case back to Judge Judd for further proceedings. Four days after that ruling, Federal Judge John Dooling decided Orlando's case. This time, the political question doctrine did not stand in the way.

Judge Dooling denied Orlando's motion for a preliminary injunction on grounds that would be repeated by other courts which reviewed the underlying merits of these challenges to the Vietnam War. Dooling found that Orlando's "deployment orders were constitutionally authorized, because Congress, by 'appropriating the nation's treasure and conscripting its manpower,' had 'furnished forth the sinew of war' and because 'the reality of the collaborative action of the executive and the legislative required by the Constitution has been present from the earliest stages.'"[142]

Berk's case eventually reached the federal appeals court again together with Orlando's appeal. The appeals court reiterated its position that the political question doctrine did not bar judicial review of this constitutional claim.

> We held in the first Berk opinion that the constitutional delegation of the war-declaring power to the Congress contains a discoverable and manageable standard imposing on the Congress a duty of mutual participation in the prosecution of war. Judicial scrutiny of that duty, therefore, is not foreclosed by the political question doctrine.[143]

"As we see it," the court continued, "the test is whether there is any action by the Congress sufficient to authorize or ratify the military action in question."[144]

Turning to the merits, the court found that Congress had taken such action. "Congress has ratified the executive's initiatives by appropriating billions of dollars to carry out military operations in Southeast Asia and by extending the Military Selective Service Act with full knowledge that persons conscripted under the Act had been, and would continue to be, sent to Vietnam."[145] The court also cited Congress's passage of the Gulf of Tonkin resolution, though a later ruling from that same appeals court, following Congress's repeal of the resolution, made clear that the military appropriations and the extension of the military draft constituted "sufficient legislative action . . . to ratify and approve the measures taken by the Executive."[146]

With the *Berk* and *Orlando* breakthroughs, other courts began to address the merits of these constitutional challenges to the war. For the most part, courts that did reach the merits applied the same reasoning in finding for the government, arguing that the military appropriations and the extension of the military amounted to action equivalent to meet Congress's responsibilities under the War Powers Clause of the Constitution. There were, however, three notable exceptions.

Three months after Judge Dooling's ruling in Orlando, a federal district court judge in California issued a lengthy opinion that moved closer to a ruling declaring the war in Vietnam to be unconstitutional. In a case brought by three members of the U.S. Military Reserves and one registrant eligible for the draft, Federal District Court Judge William T. Sweigert identified clearly the legal question presented to the court: "It must be borne in mind that the issue here is not whether our involvement in Vietnam has been necessary, wise or moral. . . . The only issue now before this court is the different, narrow, legal question whether, regardless of the necessity, wisdom or morality of the war, it is being waged by and under the authority of the branch of our government in which such power is constitutionally vested."[147] While denying standing to the plaintiff eligible for the draft, Judge Sweigert refused to deny standing to the three members of the U.S. Military Reserves. "To say that these three plaintiffs must wait until they are called up, perhaps suddenly, and ordered to the

Vietnam area, perhaps quickly, and then file a court suit for a declaration of their legal rights, perhaps with too little time to do so, borders, we think, on the absurd."[148]

Judge Sweigert also refused to dismiss the case on political question grounds. Referring to the Supreme Court's ruling in the Youngstown case during the Korean War, he wrote that "to strike down as unconstitutional a President's wartime seizure of a few private steel mills but to shy away on 'political question' grounds from interfering with a presidential war, itself, would be to strain at a gnat and swallow a camel."[149] Judge Sweigert surveyed the history of litigation over the Vietnam War and highlighted Judge Dooling's opinion as the only ruling, at that point, that had reached the merits. "Whatever the ultimate decision on the merits of the constitutional question may be," he continued, "we are of the opinion that the courts, eschewing indecision, inaction, or avoidance on such grounds as 'no standing,' 'sovereign immunity,' and 'political question,' should discharge their traditional responsibility for interpreting the Constitution of the United States."[150]

Unlike Judge Dooling, however, Judge Sweigert appeared to lean against the argument that Congress had authorized the war through the passage of military appropriations and an extension of the military draft.

[A] strong case can be made for the proposition that compliance with the Constitution of the United States and its plain provision that the power to declare war lies, not in the President, but in the Congress, should be made to rest upon something better than the ambivalences of congressional inaction or mere defense legislation, appropriations and questionable resolutions; that such compliance calls for nothing less than what the Constitution plainly says—a declaration of war by the Congress or at least an equally explicit congressional expression. . . . "[151]

At the conclusion of his opinion, Judge Sweigert, while denying the plaintiffs' request for an injunction, indicated that he would be ready, in the near future, to rule on the plaintiffs' request for a declaratory judgment from the court on the legality of the war. He ordered the defendants to file their answer to the plaintiffs' complaint.

The federal government sought to quickly move the case out of Judge Sweigert's courtroom. It filed an immediate and rare appeal on a denial of a motion to dismiss with the U.S. Court of Appeals for the Ninth Circuit. (When a defendant loses a motion to dismiss, an appeals court will usually not review that ruling immediately, but will rather wait until a district court issues a final judgment in the case.) In July 1972, nearly two years after Judge Sweigert's decision, the federal appeals court issued its ruling, finding that the three members of the U.S. Military Reserves did not have standing to bring their constitutional claims. It reversed Judge Sweigert's ruling and ordered him to dismiss the case.[152]

In March 1973, another federal appeals court, this time in Washington, D.C., distinguished itself when reviewing a constitutional challenge to the Vietnam War. A two-judge majority on a panel refuted the argument, applied by other courts, "that the appropriation, draft extension, and cognate laws enacted with direct or indirect reference to the Indo-China war" amounted to "a constitutionally permissible form of assent."[153] The judges wrote:

> This court cannot be unmindful of what every schoolboy knows: that in voting to appropriate money or to draft men a Congressman is not necessarily approving of the continuation of a war no matter how specifically the appropriation or draft act refers to that war. A Congressman wholly opposed to the war's commencement and continuation might vote for the military appropriations and for the draft measures because he was unwilling to abandon without support men already fighting. An honorable, decent, compassionate act of aiding those already in peril is no proof of consent to the actions that placed and continued them in that dangerous posture.[154]

The judges, however, refused to take the next step and declare that President Nixon was in violation of the War Powers Clause. They argued that, "[e]ven if his predecessors had exceeded their constitutional authority," Nixon might need time "to bring the war to an end" and whether he was proceeding in that direction was a political question unfit for judicial review.[155] The war commander and his subordinates, once again, escaped accountability.

The greatest exception to a pattern of judicial inaction during the war in Southeast Asia came from Judge Judd, the same district court judge who had heard the Berk case. By the time *Holtzman v. Schlesinger* reached Judge Judd's courtroom in April 1973, the Paris cease-fire agreements had been signed, the United States had withdrawn all ground combat troops from Vietnam, and the last known U.S. prisoners of war had been released.[156] Congresswoman Elizabeth Holtzman of New York filed suit to stop the bombing of Cambodia, a military operation that, in the month of March 1973 alone, involved hundreds of U.S. warplanes dropping 39,500 tons of explosives on the country.[157] The bombing campaign, which had begun in secret prior to Nixon and Kissinger's launch of an invasion of Cambodia in the spring of 1970, would ultimately claim hundreds of thousands of civilian lives and cause millions to become refugees.[158]

On July 25, 1973, Judge Judd issued an injunction against the defendant Secretary of Defense James Schlesinger and other defendants preventing them "from participating in any way in military activities in or over Cambodia or releasing any bombs which may fall in Cambodia."[159] Judge Judd ruled that "'there is no existing Congressional authority to order military forces into combat in Cambodia or to release bombs over Cambodia, and that military activities in Cambodia by American armed forces are unauthorized and unlawful."[160] The judge postponed the effective date of the injunction to 4:00 P.M. on July 27, 1973, to allow the government time to apply to the federal appeals court for a stay pending appeal of the injunction.[161]

Judge Judd's ruling shocked the political establishment and sparked a flurry of extraordinary activity at the appellate and Supreme Court level. The government immediately filed its motion for a stay of the injunction before the federal appeals court in New York. A panel of the appeals court heard oral argument on the motion on the morning of July 27, 1973, and granted the stay that day, setting the time for argument on the appeal for August 13, 1973.[162]

The attorneys for the plaintiffs, Holtzman and four Air Force officers on active duty who had joined the case after its filing, rushed to try to reverse the stay and allow the injunction to take effect. They filed a petition before Supreme Court Justice Thurgood Marshall. On August 1, 1973, Marshall refused to vacate the stay.[163] They then took the unusual step of refiling their petition with another justice, one who had been a constant voice of dissent in the Supreme Court's refusal to hear a constitutional challenge to the war. With the Court in recess for the summer, they found Justice Douglas in Goose Prairie, Washington State.[164] On August 3, 1973, Justice Douglas held a hearing on the petition in Yakima, Washington, and that same day he issued an order vacating the stay.

"It has become popular to think the President has that power to declare war," wrote Douglas in an opinion released the following morning. "But there is not a word in the Constitution that grants that power to him. It runs only to Congress."[165] The government had claimed that Congress had authorized the bombing by agreeing to hold off until August 15, 1973, any action cutting off funds that financed the military operation. The agreement, known as the August 15 Compromise, came under the threat of a presidential veto that would have put a halt to general appropriations, the net effect being "a temporary shutdown of vital federal activities."[166] Douglas referenced that claim and wrote that "[i]f the acts in question are so construed the result would be, as the District Court said, that the number of votes needed to sustain a presidential veto—one-third plus one—would be all that was needed to bring into operation the new and awesome power of a President to declare war."[167] "The merits of the present controversy," Douglas concluded, "are, therefore to say the least, substantial, since denial of the application before me would catapult our airmen as well as Cambodian peasants into the death zone. I do what I think any judge would do in a capital case—vacate the stay entered by the Court of Appeals."[168]

Later that day, Justice Marshall reinstated the stay.[169] He stated in his order that he had been in communication with the seven other Supreme Court justices and that they agreed with his action.[170] Justice Douglas issued a dissent, highlighting that federal law requires that the Court can act only when six of its members are present.[171] He stated that Justice Marshall's action, following a "telephonic disposition" of the issue with the other members of the Court, was "not a lawful order."[172] "Under the law as it is written," Douglas wrote, "the order of Mr. Justice Marshall of August 4, 1973, will in time be reversed by that Higher Court which invariably sits in judgment on the decisions of this Court."[173]

Four days later, the federal appeals court, having further expedited its hearing of the appeal, reversed Judge Judd's ruling. A two-judge majority found that the plaintiffs' case was barred by the political question doctrine and stated further that, even if it were able to review the merits, the August 15 Compromise served as evidence that Congress had authorized the bombing.[174] Judge Oakes of the federal appeals court dissented, stating that he could not find "any express congressional authorization for such a continuation of the Cambodian bombing."[175] He concluded with a focus on the framers' intent.

> If we return to fundamentals, as I think we must in the case of any conflict of view between the other two Branches of Government, it will be recalled that the Founding Fathers deliberately eschewed the example of the British Monarchy in which was lodged the authority to declare war and to raise and regulate fleets and armies. Rather, these powers were deliberately given to the Legislative Branch of the new American Republic in Article I, Section 8 of the Constitution.[176]

The Supreme Court refused to hear the case.

Two hundred miles north of Judge Judd's courtroom, a federal district court judge in Boston heard a similar constitutional challenge that summer to the bombing of Cambodia. On August 8, 1973, the same day as the federal appeals court ruling in the *Holtzman* case, Judge Joseph Tauro dismissed the challenge on political question grounds. Judge Tauro stated that "a federal court may judge the propriety of war activities of the executive and legislative branches only when there is a clear conflict between the actions taken by them."[177] In other words, according to Judge Tauro's analysis, if Congress is silent while the president proceeds to unlawfully declare war against another nation, the judiciary is powerless to act.

Thirty years later, Judge Tauro was assigned to hear *John Doe I v. President Bush.*

Chapter Four **The Court Is in Recess**

"Sit down everybody" (Appendix Two, p. 98).

Judge Tauro had entered the courtroom. We were all still standing as he walked up the few stairs to his chair to preside over the oral argument in *John Doe I v. President Bush*. Judges are usually found at a slightly higher elevation than everybody else in their courtrooms. The not-so-subtle message is sent to all who are present that the judge is to be respected, that the court is to be honored. That message is also sent by the requirement that everybody rise when the judge enters the courtroom. Most of the time, the clerk of the court will say, "You may be seated," as the judge takes his or her seat. Tauro was not going to wait for that. He was ready to get going.

With more than 100,000 U.S. troops already deployed to the Persian Gulf, Tauro posed his first question a few minutes into my argument. How could we be certain, he asked, that war was imminent (Appendix Two, pp. 100-101)? Unlike the Vietnam War cases, *John Doe I v. President Bush* was filed prior to the initiation of a war. Congress's exclusive war-making powers are the clearest at that point. And before an unconstitutional war has started, the judiciary's responsibility cannot be obscured by arguments about the political nature of battlefield decisions.

But a different argument is raised—that the matter is not "ripe" for judicial review, that the facts are not yet present clearly enough to warrant judicial intervention. The United States Justice Department, representing President Bush and Secretary Rumsfeld, made the ripeness argument in Tauro's courtroom. In papers that Justice Department attorneys filed in court on February 20, 2003, four weeks prior to the launch of the invasion, they stated that "[a] diplomatic or other non-military resolution of the Iraqi resolution remains a real possibility. . . . "[178] Unknown to the public at the time, the Bush administration, in early February, had initiated a secret closed bidding process among a handful of politically-connected U.S. companies for lucrative government contracts to rebuild Iraq following the war.[179] Despite the Justice Department's representation to the court, the White House, by late February, was well into its march toward the conquering and occupation of Iraq.

Prior to the first Persian Gulf War, a federal district court judge in Washington dismissed, on ripeness grounds, a constitutional challenge brought to that war.[180] Federal Judge Harold H. Greene made clear that the case, known as *Dellums v. Bush,* was not barred by the political question doctrine. "[T]he Court," Greene wrote, "is not prepared to read out of the Constitution the clause granting to the Congress, and to it alone, the authority 'to declare war.'"[181] Yet the plaintiffs in the Dellums case only included members of Congress. As such, Greene focused on the fact that they did not represent a majority of the members. He found that "unless the Congress as a whole, or by a majority, is heard from, the controversy here cannot be deemed ripe; it is only if the majority of the Congress seeks relief from an infringement on its constitutional war-declaration power that it may be entitled to receive it."[182] Were there to have been U.S. soldier-plaintiffs in the case, Greene might have issued a different ripeness analysis. In any case, President George H. W. Bush did seek and receive congressional authorization for that war following Greene's ruling and prior to the launch of that war.

In our reply brief filed prior to oral argument, we answered the ripeness claim by emphasizing to Judge Tauro the presence of U.S. soldier-plaintiffs in *Doe v. Bush.* We highlighted that delay in judicial intervention "would cause unconscionable hardship to the military plaintiffs and their families."[183] We also pointed out that the government could not have it both ways. In the *Dellums* case, the government argued that the plaintiffs' claims were not ripe. In a 1984 case brought after the invasion of Grenada had begun, the government argued that the plaintiffs' claims were moot—too late.[184] "Under this flawed rationale," we stated, "there is never a time when the plaintiffs' claims in this case could be timely."[185]

During our oral argument before Tauro, we focused on another key difference between *Doe v. Bush* and the *Dellums* case. On February 13, 2003, the day we filed the case, the *Washington Post* ran a story with the headline, "U.S. troops in Iraq: War's initial ground phase is under way."[186] The newspaper reported that U.S. Special Operations troops were "already operating in various parts of Iraq, hunting for weapons sites, establishing a communications network and seeking potential defectors from Iraqi military units in what amounts to the initial ground phase of a war. . . ."[187] The article cited two unnamed U.S. military officials "with direct knowledge" of the troops' activities.[188] They told the *Washington Post* that the troops had been "in and out of Iraq for well over a month" and that they were "laying the groundwork for conventional U.S. forces that could quickly seize large portions of Iraq if President Bush gives a formal order to go to war. . . ."[189]

At the time, the White House had still managed to keep secret the fact that a small number of major U.S. companies had been invited to participate in a bidding process for hundreds of millions of dollars in government contracts to rebuild Iraq. The story, however, of U.S. Special Operations troops operating in Iraq in January and February, had become public. Our case was as ripe as it was ever going to be.

Judge Tauro quickly moved to the political question doctrine and the standard that he had applied in the Cambodia bombing case of *Drinan v. Nixon* thirty years earlier. "Doesn't there have to be resolute conflict before the Court has jurisdiction?" he asked. "Otherwise it's a political question" (Appendix Two, p. 105).

In preparing for the oral argument, we were well aware of the likelihood that Tauro would focus on his ruling in the *Drinan* case. We sought to address that ruling in two ways. First, we argued that congressional silence is not equivalent to a congressional declaration of war as required by the Constitution. The October resolution had unlawfully delegated to the president the decision of whether or not to send the nation into war. Congress had, in effect, decided to remain silent. The judiciary has a duty to intervene when the political branches are in conflict, but that same judiciary must also intervene when the political branches are in collusion to violate the Constitution.

We made an alternative argument, as well, one that met the "resolute conflict" standard. We argued the October resolution, if it were to be read as authorizing a war against Iraq, conditioned that authorization on the president obtaining approval from the United Nations Security Council. We stated that the language of the October resolution and the legislative history behind it supported that alternative reading. As such, Congress and the president were in direct conflict on this matter of war and peace. Congress said that we could go to war only with U.N. approval. The president was preparing to go it alone.

Tauro did not respond to these arguments. He seemed ready to move on.

Joseph Hunt, a Justice Department attorney, presented the government's argument. Hunt argued that the case should be dismissed on political question grounds, that there was no conflict between the executive and legislative branches. On the question of ripeness, Hunt stated that "nobody . . . in this courtroom knows whether or not the President of the United States will commit United States Armed Forces to an attack, a military attack against Iraq" (Appendix Two, p. 117).

Then Hunt made a sweeping and extraordinary claim. "The Constitution," Hunt asserted, "doesn't say that the President must first wait for Congress to declare war" (Appendix Two, p. 118). The Justice Department was trying to transform the president's narrow power to repel a sudden attack, absent a congressional declaration of war, into a new, sweeping, unilateral power to launch a preemptive first-strike war against another nation. "[I]rrespective of any Congressional assent," the president's attorneys wrote in their brief, "the President has broad powers as Commander in Chief of the Armed Forces under the Constitution that would justify the use of force in Iraq."[190] Such a claim of executive power to initiate a war directly contravened the framers' intent when they crafted the War Powers Clause. There was no legal precedent in the more than two centuries of case law to substantiate this assertion of power.

Tauro did not ask Hunt any questions. He was silent throughout the presentation. In my rebuttal, Tauro reiterated his view that there needed to be a "resolute conflict" between the two political branches before a court could intervene on a war powers question (Appendix Two, p. 121). He allowed time for additional rebuttal by Hunt, and then announced that the court would be in recess for one hour after which he would return to issue his decision.

The writing was on the wall. Tauro had his mind made up before the hearing started. As far as he was concerned, we were just going through the motions.

One hour later, Tauro read his ruling from the bench (Appendix Two, pp. 127-130) denying the plaintiffs' motion for an injunction and granting the government's motion to dismiss.[191] He stuck to his reasoning from thirty years ago. Without "resolute conflict" between the Congress and the president, he would not intervene.[192] He asserted that "[c]ase law makes clear that Congress does not have the exclusive right to determine whether or not the United States will engage in war,"[193] but he cited no case law for this proposition. In fact, Tauro cited only two court opinions in his three-page ruling: the 1973 *Drinan v. Nixon* case, which he decided, and the federal appeals court ruling in *Holtzman v. Schlesinger* which was decided on the same day of that year. The legal sanction for the bombing of Cambodia served as Tauro's sole authority and precedent in justification of President Bush's preemptive invasion of Iraq.

Within hours of Tauro's ruling, we filed a notice of appeal and a motion for expedited review before the federal appeals court in Boston. By the next morning, the appeals court had granted the motion, placing the appeal on a rare, fast-track schedule with oral argument before a three-judge panel set for that following week. Tauro's ruling would not be the last word from a court before the launch of an invasion.

Chapter Five **Questions for Both Sides**

Diland Herbert had been late to his immigration hearing. It had been raining heavily that day in January 2002, and Herbert had worried about taking his sick child on the walk to the subway station in Dorchester for the ride into downtown Boston. He and his girlfriend, the child's mother, had called a cab to take them directly to the immigration court. By the time they had arrived, it was too late. The immigration judge had ordered Herbert deported in his absence. Herbert, who came to this country from Trinidad and Tobago in 1976 at the age of three, now faced, at the age of twenty-nine, a deportation order for being a half-hour late.[194]

On March 4, 2003, a three-judge panel of the United States Court of Appeals for the First Circuit heard oral argument on several cases. One involved a dispute as to the title of a boat. Another involved a question about a police search of a vehicle. Herbert's case was also argued that day. And then there was *John Doe I v. President Bush*.

The argument regarding the constitutionality of president Bush's planned military invasion of Iraq was to come at the end of the morning session. It was only fitting that Herbert's appeal would precede it. The fact that a federal appeals court would have to review a case involving a twenty-six-year legal resident of the United States facing deportation for being a half-hour late to his immigration hearing placed the *Doe v. Bush* case in the context of our times.

Judge Sandra L. Lynch started the questioning in our appeal. Lynch, who chaired the panel, asked whether ours was a "magic-words argument," an argument that Congress must utter the words "declaration of war" in order to satisfy the mandate of Article I, Section 8 of the Constitution (Appendix Three, p. 135). "[A]bsolutely not," I answered. Congress may either declare war "or take any other equivalent action" in order to comply with its constitutional responsibilities (Appendix Three, p. 135). The October resolution does not serve as equivalent action. "It transfers to the President the decision of whether or not this nation is to be sent into war" (Appendix Three, p. 135).

Lynch then referred to the section of the October resolution requiring the president to report back to the Congress within forty-eight hours of launching a military invasion against Iraq. At that point, she said, Congress "presumably could then either declare a war or give further authorization or say this is contrary to our intent" (Appendix Three, pp. 135–136).

"[T]his gets strictly to the framers' intent," I replied, ". . . which was to ensure that both houses of Congress participate in a declaration of war . . . The constitutional default position is that we're not at war." (Appendix Three, p. 136). The only way we can get to war, in accordance with the Constitution, is if both the United States Senate and the United States House of Representatives vote to send us to war. If either the Senate or the House votes against going to war, then the country cannot go to war. Thus, the president cannot go to Congress after unlawfully starting a war and require that both houses of Congress vote against war in order to stop it. "The default position is we're not at war and before we go to war, Congress must vote" (Appendix Three, p. 136).

Judge Norman Stahl joined the questioning. He focused on language in the October resolution that referred to the War Powers Resolution passed by Congress in 1973 as the war in Southeast Asia came to an end. Does not that language indicate that Congress "was giving the President the go-ahead?" Stahl asked (Appendix Three, p. 137).

The reference to the War Powers Resolution, I answered, cannot detract from the language in which Congress unlawfully transfers to the president the decision of whether or not to start a war (Appendix Three, pp. 137, 140).

Judge Conrad Cyr then interjected: "So, if we were to accept the first prong of your argument, which is to the effect that the Congress cannot simply say, 'You have the authority whenever you decide to exercise it,' . . . in your view that can't work as long as the President doesn't act immediately?" (Appendix Three, pp. 137-138).

The question sharpened the focus of our claim. "Your honor, the issue isn't 'You can do it whenever you want.' The issue is 'if you want.'" (Appendix Three, p. 138). I said that had been made all the more clear by a President who has repeatedly stated, "'I'll decide whether or not to send this nation to war'" (Appendix Three, p. 138).

What about the president's responsibilities as commander in chief, Cyr queried. "The Commander-in-Chief responsibilities," I said, "do not involve declaring war. . . . " (Appendix Three, p. 138).

The questioning continued. This was an active bench. At one point, Stahl asked whether we saw any circumstances "short of a declaration of war by Congress where the Executive can put troops into the field?" "Absolutely," I answered, ". . . to repel a sudden attack" (Appendix Three, p. 140).

"Well how do you get to Kosovo?" Stahl responded (Appendix Three, p. 140). In March 1999, President William Jefferson Clinton had ordered U.S. participation in the NATO bombing of Kosovo, Yugoslavia. The bombing campaign occurred in the absence of a congressional declaration of war and in the absence of a sudden attack on the United States or an ally. Thirty-one members of Congress had filed suit against President Clinton "seeking a declaratory judgment that the President's use of American forces against Yugoslavia was unlawful under both the War Powers Clause of the Constitution and the War Powers Resolution."[195] In February 2000, months after the bombing campaign had ended, a federal appeals court in Washington ruled that the members of Congress did not have standing to bring their claim.[196] Judge David Tatel, however, had issued an important concurring opinion stating that "were this case brought by plaintiffs with standing, we could determine whether the President, in undertaking the air campaign in Yugoslavia, exceeded his authority under the Constitution or the War Powers Resolution."[197] The political question doctrine, Tatel had written, does not bar judicial review of such a claim.

I answered Judge Stahl's question that the Kosovo bombing violated the Constitution "and the fact that prior violations have occurred doesn't change the fact this violation is about to occur. . . . " I added that this violation was even worse than the Kosovo bombing as it involved a premeditated invasion, conquest, and occupation of another country on a scale that was without precedent in the history of the United States (Appendix Three, p. 141).

Judge Stahl then asked the toughest question posed to our side that morning. "Assume for the moment that the Executive had absolutely excellent information that missiles are about to be launched against the United States," Stahl said. "Does the Executive have any first-strike capability under those circumstances?" (Appendix Three, p. 141).

We had discussed this question in our moot session the prior day. "It depends on what the 'about to' is," I replied. "We would argue here, your honor, that time permits. Time permits for the President to go back to Congress. He can do it today. Congress can have an immediate debate. It isn't the same situation. The facts of this case clearly permit Congress to debate and declare whether or not we're going to war. If this were an emergency, then we would be at war already, and we're not" (Appendix Three, pp. 141–142).

Unlike the hearing before Judge Tauro, the appellate

panel was as equally engaged in questioning the Justice Department's attorney. Gregory G. Katsas, a deputy assistant attorney general, handled the appellate argument for the government. Katsas had attended the hearing before Judge Tauro a week earlier. Within minutes after Tauro issued his ruling from the bench, Katsas had descended to the lobby of the federal courthouse to read a statement to reporters from United States Attorney General John Ashcroft. Ashcroft had proclaimed that Tauro's ruling showed that the Congress and the president were united and that the current war push was in keeping with the Constitution.

Katsas began his argument by reiterating Tauro's ruling that the plaintiffs' claims were barred by the political question doctrine. Judge Stahl interrupted early into the argument, asking: "Do you see any place where the judiciary would come in play in this scenario?" (Appendix Three, p. 147). Katsas responded that it was "very hard to imagine." He suggested that because Congress held the power of whether to finance a military operation, the system of checks and balances worked without judicial intervention (Appendix Three, p. 147).

Judge Lynch made the question even more direct. She presented a hypothetical in which Congress and the president were in conflict on whether to go to war and Congress had passed a resolution telling the president that he was in violation of the congressional mandate. "[W]ould you say," she asked Katsas, "that courts which normally determine statutory interpretation questions are required to stay out of that?" (Appendix Three, pp. 147–148). Katsas said yes, arguing that the political question doctrine is not about timing but about subject matters (Appendix Three, p. 148).

"Well, that's one reading of it," Lynch shot back. "There's another reading of it—that it is a doctrine of restraint with about half a dozen reasons for it that sometimes prevail, sometimes don't. In *Bush versus Gore,* it certainly didn't prevail" (Appendix Three, p. 148). Lynch's point made sense. The political question doctrine did not seem to bar the Supreme Court from stopping the counting of ballots in Florida in December 2000 and selecting George W. Bush as president.

Katsas moved away from the hypothetical and returned to the government's argument that the October resolution constituted "a very expressed and unambiguous statement of approval by Congress" (Appendix Three, p. 149).

But Stahl quickly put forward a different scenario. "If we didn't have the war power statute," Stahl said, referring to the War Powers Resolution of 1973, ". . . and the President decided, under the circumstances that are facing the country today as he sees them, that a war against Iraq was necessary, does he have the authority under the Constitution to make that determination without congressional action?" (Appendix Three, pp. 150–151).

Here, Katsas revealed the true colors of President Bush's sweeping claim of inherent executive power. "He does," Katsas said, "but, as a practical matter, he couldn't prosecute the hostilities or the war without resources" (Appendix Three, p. 151).

The claim is so breathtaking it needs to be repeated. Stahl had just asked the president's lawyer whether, according to the Constitution, the president could launch a preemptive war against Iraq without any congressional approval. The president's lawyer had answered yes. And so the distinction between president and king had become further blurred.

"Wait a minute," Stahl responded, sounding astonished. "He's got resources in hand today, he's got a lot of troops overseas now . . . and he hasn't asked for appropriation, as I understand it, yet for the war. And he's got them over there and decides to put them into battle. Historically, Congress has never undercut our troops once that happens. Doesn't that make the argument that Congress has the appropriation authority sort of illusory?" (Appendix Three, p.150).

"I don't think so," Katsas said. "That's the check. . . . " (Appendix Three, p. 151). Katsas did not answer Stahl's point that the president already had the resources in hand and had already sent a massive invading force to the borders of Iraq—all without any congressional appropriation. He continued: "The President has the power of the sword—" (Appendix Three, p. 151).

Lynch interrupted him, refuting that it is "an exclusive power to the exclusion of all other remedies" (Appendix Three, pp. 151–152). Lynch, clearly trying to see if the president's position had any limits, then advanced another hypothetical. "Suppose Congress were to pass a resolution that said, without prior conditions, the President can commence a war anywhere, anytime he wants. That, at least on the face of it, does seem to be a transfer of congressional power to the Executive Branch." Lynch asked Katsas whether he would argue that such a resolution could not be reviewed by a court and, if it could, whether he would argue that it was constitutional (Appendix Three, p. 152).

Sensing perhaps that the judges were catching on to the extreme nature of his argument, Katsas tried to cloud his answer. With respect to the first question, Katsas said that he would "need to know more" (Appendix Three, p. 152). He would argue that the matter could not be reviewed by a court if, after the president made a commitment to initiate military action, Congress "did nothing to manifest disagreement" (Appendix Three, p. 152). Yet Lynch's hypothetical presented precisely this scenario involving congressional silence. The president's attorney dodged the question.

As to the second question, Katsas "concede[d] that the power to declare war, whatever that may be, is non-delegable" (Appendix Three, p. 152). He then quickly returned, however, to the issue of whether such a dispute is "judicially resolvable" (Appendix Three, p. 152). In other words, according to the president's lawyer, even if Congress had unlawfully delegated to the president the power to start a war at anytime, anywhere, no court could likely intervene to protect and uphold the Constitution.

At that point, Katsas applied the classic strategy used by an extremist when backed into a corner. He diverted attention away from his argument and labeled the plaintiffs' argument "breathtakingly radical" (Appendix Three, p. 152). He asserted that the War Powers Resolution of 1973 "unconstitutionally infringes executive power" (Appendix Three, p. 152). In November 1973, Congress passed the War Powers Resolution,[198] over President Richard Nixon's veto, in the wake of the nation's disillusionment with the Vietnam War. The War Powers Resolution reiterated the framers' intent with Article I, Section 8, and established requirements for presidential reporting to the Congress in the event of the deployment of U.S. armed forces. We had argued that, whatever the case, the War Powers Resolution (a statute passed by Congress) could not trump the War Powers Clause of the Constitution (the Constitution being the supreme law of the land). Katsas sought to recast our argument as one that the War Powers Resolution "is unconstitutional because it doesn't go far enough" (Appendix Three, p. 153).

There, in a matter of twenty minutes, was the president's argument, as enunciated by his representative in a federal courtroom on the eve of war. The court, according to the president, was powerless to act, under this circumstance or nearly any other circumstance. The warning Katsas brought to these three federal judges was clear: Do not get in the way of this president's march toward war.

Chapter Six **Just the Facts**

The day after the federal appeals court hearing, seventy-four law professors from around the country filed a friend-of-the-court brief in support of the plaintiffs in *Doe v. Bush*. The law professors wrote that "[t]he exercise of judicial authority is here urgently needed ..." and compared the case to the 1952 case of *Youngstown Sheet & Tube Co. v. Sawyer,* in which the Supreme Court intervened to stop President Truman's seizure of the steel mills during the Korean War.[199] "It is difficult to imagine," the law professors continued "a situation presenting separation of powers questions more narrowly and inviting judicial intervention more urgently than does the present case."[200]

The following week the court issued its ruling, refusing to intervene.

But it left the door open.

With respect to our argument that Congress had unlawfully transferred to the president the power to declare war, the court stated that the delegation in the October resolution did not "raise a sufficiently clear constitutional issue."[201] The court contrasted the case with the Supreme Court's 1998 ruling in *Clinton v. City of New York*, striking down the Line Item Veto Act passed by Congress.[202] The act had unlawfully given to the president the power to veto specific lines of a budget, transforming the presidential veto power into an illegal power by the executive to appropriate money. We had cited that ruling in our legal briefs as involving a recent example of Congress unconstitutionally delegating to the president a power (to make appropriations) reserved only for Congress. The appeals court said that our case differed from *Clinton* in "the scale of the purported delegation."[203] "The Line Item Veto Act gave the President wide discretion to cancel items of discretionary budget authority, direct spending, or limited tax benefits. The determinations required of the President in the October Resolution are much more narrowly focused."[204] The court claimed that Congress's transfer to the president of the decision of whether or not to launch a first-strike war against Iraq was on a smaller scale than the transfer to the president of appropriations decisions.

The court also argued that the case involved shared powers between the Congress and the president. "To the Congress goes the power to declare war. . . . The President's role as commander-in-chief is one of the few executive powers enumerated by the Constitution."[205] To back up this argument, the court cited a previous ruling by the First Circuit Court of Appeals during the Vietnam War, which had stated that the Constitution overall "envisages the joint participation of the Congress and the executive in determining the scale and duration of hostilities."[206] But the determination of "the scale and duration of hostilities" cannot be equated to the determination of whether or not to start a war. The latter power is not shared by the president. It is held exclusively by the United States Congress, as the framers intended more than two centuries ago. The appeals court ignored that crucial distinction.

The court led its analysis, however, with a focus on our alternative argument—that if the October resolution did authorize war, such authorization could only be read as conditioned on approval by the United Nations Security Council. With respect to this argument, we had pointed to the language in the resolution referencing the enforcement of "all relevant United Nations Security Council resolutions regarding Iraq."[207] The United Nations—and not the United States, we had said, is responsible for enforcing its own resolutions. The United States, therefore, needed U.N. approval to enforce such a mandate. We had also pointed to the legislative history in which numerous members of Congress had stated that they were voting for the October resolution to strengthen the president's hand at the United Nations for a multilateral operation.

The appeals court ruled that the issue presented by this alternative argument was not yet fit for judicial review.[208]

"Many important questions," the court stated, "remain unanswered about whether there will be a war, and, if so, under what conditions. . . . As events unfold, it may become clear that diplomacy has either succeeded or failed decisively. The Security Council, now divided on the issue, may reach a consensus."[209] "To evaluate this claim now," the court continued, ". . . [w]e would need to assume that the Security Council will not authorize war, and that the President will proceed nonetheless."[210]

This court ruling was met with silence from the United States Justice Department. This time, no statement was issued by Attorney General Ashcroft. Reporters wrote that the Justice Department refused to comment.

The court had issued an invitation to consider the matter again if such facts became more defined. And they did.

The court issued its ruling on Thursday, March 13, 2003. By that Sunday, March 16, President Bush, British Prime Minister Tony Blair, and Spanish Prime Minister Jose Maria Aznar held a summit in the Azores off of Portugal. At a joint news conference following their meeting, the president said: "Tomorrow is the day we determine whether or not diplomacy can work."[211] He made it clear that he would make a final effort that Monday to obtain United Nations Security Council approval for a military invasion of Iraq, and if he did not gain that approval, he would go it alone. News organizations that Sunday began reporting that the president would issue an ultimatum on Monday evening in a televised address to the nation.

The following Monday morning it became clear that the president did not have the votes on the Security Council to approve his war. The White House withdrew its proposed Security Council resolution. United Nations inspectors began an immediate evacuation of Iraq, and the United States State Department ordered the departure of diplomats' family members and non-emergency personnel from its embassies and consulates in Israel, Kuwait, and Syria. War was clearly imminent.

With the emergence of these facts, we returned to the federal appeals court that Monday afternoon with an emergency petition to reconsider the court's ruling. We argued that the plaintiffs' claim was now ripe for the court's review. In its March 13 opinion, the appeals court had stated that its conclusion did not mean that challenges such as that of the plaintiffs "would never be ripe for decision before military action began."[212] "If, however, in light of the ripening of the circumstances in this case," we wrote, "this Court were still to decline to reach the merits of Plaintiffs' claim, it would essentially be conceding that courts may never review these matters before military action begins."[213] "The President's plans for imminent military action," we continued, "are in direct conflict with the conditions set by the United States Congress in the October Resolution and demand immediate judicial intervention."[214]

The next day the appeals court issued a one-paragraph order denying our petition. The court acknowledged that "some of the contingencies described in our opinion appear to have been resolved. . . . " but claimed that "others have not."[215] Then, applying circular reasoning, the court stated: "Most importantly, Congress has taken no action which presents a 'fully developed dispute between the two elected branches.'"[216]

The ruling made no sense. We had argued that the president and the Congress stood opposed in a clear dispute. The October resolution—to be read as constitutional—authorized the president to wage war against Iraq only if he obtained United Nations Security Council approval. The president had demonstrated that he would violate that congressional mandate and launch a war without Security Council approval. The very facts the court had said were missing on March 13 to create a dispute between the political branches had emerged four days later. But now the court ignored its March 13 opinion and said there was still no dispute.

The court lacked the courage to carry out its own ruling. When faced with the precise scenario that it said it would need to evaluate the plaintiffs' claim, these three judges backed away. Perhaps they had thought diplomacy might still work. Perhaps they had hoped the White House would follow a different course as a result of their March 13 opinion. Perhaps they had believed that the plaintiffs would not return to their courtroom. Perhaps the warning from the Justice Department's Katsas had gotten to them.

Whatever the case, we had reached the end of the road. The following night, the president launched his invasion of Iraq. The Constitution had been suspended.

Chapter Seven

**The Preemptive
War Doctrine and
the Constitution**

On Sunday, May 11, 2003, the *Washington Post* ran a head-line on its front page: "Frustrated, U.S. Arms Team to Leave Iraq: Task Force Unable to Find Any Weapons."[217] The news-paper reported that the 75th Exploitation Task Force of the United States Army, "[t]he group directing all known U.S. search efforts for weapons of mass destruction in Iraq," was "winding down operations without finding proof that Pres-ident Saddam Hussein kept clandestine stocks of outlawed arms."[218] The article quoted Army Col. Richard McPhee, a leader of the task force, as saying: "My unit has not found chemical weapons. . . . That's a fact. And I'm forty-seven years old, having a birthday in one of Saddam Hussein's palaces on a lake in the middle of Baghdad. It's surreal. The whole thing is surreal."[219] Referring to the weapons of mass destruction, McPhee said: "Do I know where they are? I wish I did . . . but we will find them. Or not. I don't know. I'm being honest here."[220]

Two weeks prior to this *Washington Post* article, the British newspaper, *The Independent,* reported that "intelligence agencies on both sides of the Atlantic were furious that briefings they gave political leaders were distorted in the rush to war with Iraq."[221] The newspaper quoted a "high-level U.K. source" who said: "They ignored intelligence assessments which said Iraq was not a threat."[222]

In his State of the Union speech on January 28, 2003, President Bush made a series of claims regarding Iraq's existing stockpile of weapons of mass destruction. None of them have yet proven to be true—and all evidence indicates that they never will be. He spoke of "25,000 liters of anthrax," "38,000 liters of botulinum toxin," and "500 tons of sarin, mustard, and VX nerve agent."[223] And he made that allegation, already proven to be false as based on forged documents, that Iraq had "recently sought significant quantities of uranium from Africa."[224] The president then repeated his mantra that he used throughout his march toward war: "If Saddam Hussein does not fully disarm," he said, "for the safety of our people and for the peace of the world, we will lead a coalition to disarm him."[225]

The threat of weapons of mass destruction served as the

president's declared basis for the United States' invasion of Iraq, with or without United Nations approval. The fact that no such weapons have yet to be found underscores the very reason the framers placed the War Powers Clause in the U.S. Constitution: to ensure that the president would not hold the power of a king. A king may lie and, using that lie, a king, on his own, has the power to send his kingdom into war. A president may also lie, but a president alone cannot use that lie to start a war. According to the United States Constitution, Congress alone must make that momentous decision. It must deliberate and debate, assessing all of the arguments for and against a war. If a lie is to be told which brings our troops into battle, Congress must first accept that lie and stand behind it. By allowing the president to make the determination of whether or not to launch an invasion of Iraq, as the October resolution did, Congress unlawfully allowed the president to use whatever evidence—or whatever lies—he chose as the basis for sending the nation into war.

The story of *John Doe I v. President Bush* is a story of the Constitution under attack, under attack from the president of the United States, with the collusion of Congress. In the face of this attack, a courageous group of United States citizens, including members of the United States Armed Forces, sought relief from our third branch of government, the branch on which we rely to uphold the law, to protect us from the road to tyranny. And the judiciary turned its back.

But it would be dangerous to view this story as an isolated incident. The president and his subordinates have made clear that the war against Iraq represents the implementation of a new doctrine in U.S. foreign policy—the doctrine of preemptive war. The doctrine threatens the lives of people around the world, and it threatens our Constitution.

The origins of the preemptive war doctrine can be found in a 1992 draft of a Defense Department document prepared by Paul Wolfowitz, then-Under Secretary of Defense for Policy in President George H. W. Bush's administration. Wolfowitz, who is now the Deputy Secretary of Defense, wrote that, in the post-Cold War era, the primary objective of U.S. military strategy should be "to prevent the re-emergence of a new rival."[226] The United States, in other words, should seek to maintain its position as the world's sole superpower. To preserve this superior military strength, the United States, Wolfowitz argued, should be prepared to launch preemptive military actions against other nations. And he wrote that "the United States should be postured to act independently when collective action cannot be orchestrated."[227] In other words, the United States should be prepared to go it alone. Wolfowitz focused on Iraq and North Korea as the primary case studies to make his argument.[228]

The forty-six-page draft of the document, called the "Defense Planning Guidance," was classified and, for several weeks, it moved quietly among the highest levels in the Pentagon. Then, in March 1992, the document was leaked to the *New York Times* and the *Washington Post,* creating a fury in the nation's capitol. Senator Byrd called it "myopic, shallow, and disappointing."[229] Senator Biden described it as "literally a Pax Americana."[230] According to Barton Gellman of the *Washington Post,* "[i]nside the U.S. defense planning establishment, there were people who thought this thing was nuts."[231] The White House ordered Dick Cheney, then-Secretary of Defense, to redraft it.[232] Within weeks, a new version of the document was circulated and approved. This version eliminated the theme of maintaining U.S. military superiority in the world and emphasized "the importance of strengthening international organizations like the United Nations for resolving disputes."[233] Wolfowitz's strategy had been rejected—for the time being.

In 1997, a group consisting mostly of Washington neoconservatives, created the Project for the New American Century (PNAC). Wolfowitz is considered "the ideological father of the group."[234] Other founders include now-Vice President Dick Cheney, now-Secretary of Defense Donald Rumsfeld and Richard Perle. Perle is now a member of the Defense Policy Board, a civilian body that advises the Pentagon; he was forced to resign as the Board's chairman in March 2003, following revelations that his venture capital firm stood to profit from the war in Iraq. "Above all else, PNAC desires and demands one thing: The establishment of a global American empire to bend the will of all nations."[235]

In an open letter in 1998 to President Clinton, PNAC pressed for unilateral U.S. military action against Iraq for the purpose of "removing Saddam Hussein and his regime from power."[236] "Of the eighteen people who signed the letter, ten are now in the Bush administration."[237] The letter marked a prelude to President Bush's war against Iraq.

In September 2000, PNAC distributed a paper entitled: "Rebuilding America's Defenses: Strategy, Forces and Resources for a New Century."[238] The paper aimed to resurface the strategy Wolfowitz outlined in his rejected 1992 draft for the Defense Department:

> The Defense Policy Guidance drafted in the early months of
> 1992 provided a blueprint for maintaining U.S. preeminence,
> precluding the rise of a great power rival, and shaping the
> international security order in line with American principles
> and interests. Leaked before it had been formally approved,
> the document was criticized as an effort by "cold warriors" to
> keep defense spending high and cuts in forces small despite
> the collapse of the Soviet Union; not surprisingly, it was sub-
> sequently buried by the new administration.[239]

But with two months to go before the 2000 general election
and the possibility of a return to power, Wolfowitz and others
at PNAC sought to resurrect their plan for U.S. global domi-
nation.

The 2000 PNAC report cited as a "core mission" for U.S.
military forces to "fight and decisively win multiple, simultaneous major theater wars."[240] It called for sharp increases in
U.S. defense spending and the creation of "U.S. space forces"
to control outer space.[241] It sought to acquire military control
of the Persian Gulf region, with regime change in Iraq as part
of an overall strategy.[242] It described U.S. military forces
abroad as "the cavalry on the new American frontier."[243] It
advocated "unquestioned U.S. military preeminence" in the
world.[244]

The paper argued that "[t]o preserve American military
preeminence in the coming decades, the Department of
Defense must move aggressively to experiment with new
technologies and operational concepts, and seek to exploit
the emerging revolution in military affairs."[245]

The effects of this military transformation will have profound implications for how wars are fought, what kind of weapons will dominate the battlefield and, inevitably, which nations enjoy military preeminence.[246]

And, in eerie language, the paper said: "Further, the process of transformation, even if it brings revolutionary change, is likely to be a long one, absent some catastrophic and catalyzing event—like a new Pearl Harbor."[247]

Then came September 11. Wolfowitz and his PNAC colleagues within and outside the new Bush administration seized the moment to move their agenda. Within thirty hours after the attacks of September 11, "Rumsfeld asked the President, 'Why shouldn't the U.S. go against Iraq, not just Al Qaeda?'"[248] On September 13, 2001, Wolfowitz held a briefing at the Pentagon. He said: "It will be a campaign, not a single action."[249]

I think one has to say it's not just simply a matter of capturing people and holding them accountable, but removing the sanctuaries, removing the support systems, ending states who sponsor terrorism.[250]

The "ending states" comment drew an immediate reaction. Reporters asked other Bush administration officials: What did Wolfowitz mean? Colin Powell, President Bush's Secretary of State, had served as the Chairman of the Joint Chiefs of Staff under Bush's father. At the time, he had advanced behind closed doors an alternative vision of U.S. foreign policy to the vision pushed by Wolfowitz.[251] Now, Powell was alarmed and brought his dispute into the open.

"We're after ending terrorism," Powell responded at a press conference. "And if there are states and regimes, nations that support terrorism, we hope to persuade them that it is in their interest to stop doing that. But I think ending terrorism is where I would like to leave it and let Mr. Wolfowitz speak for himself."[252]

Wolfowitz and the hawks were forced to wait a little longer. But by the following year, their strategy became the policy of the Bush administration.

On June 1, 2002, President Bush delivered the graduation speech at the United States Military Academy at West Point, New York. For the first time, a United States president embraced the idea of preemptive wars against other nations. "[O]ur security," the President said, "will require all Americans to be forward-looking and resolute, to be ready for preemptive action when necessary to defend our liberty and to defend our lives."[253] Ten days later, the Washington Post ran an article on the emergence of this new doctrine, describing it as "a radical shift from the half-century-old policies of deterrence and containment."[254]

By September 2002, the preemptive war doctrine had become a centerpiece of the president's National Security Strategy document, a document prepared periodically by every administration's National Security Council.[255] The document, in many ways, mirrored the Defense Policy Guidance draft created by Wolfowitz in 1992. Gellman of the Washington Post was one of the first to report on that classified draft. Comparing that draft with the president's National

Security Strategy, Gellman says: "[Y]ou simply have to lay the documents side by side and you will see huge areas in which they're the same. . . ."[256]

By its own terms, the preemptive war doctrine requires evidence that there is a threat to preempt. In the case of Iraq, the Bush administration argued that war was necessary to find and destroy Iraq's weapons of mass destruction. The Pentagon's new leadership, however, was not satisfied with the intelligence data on Iraq provided by the Central Intelligence Agency and even by the Pentagon's own Defense Intelligence Agency.[257] According to a May 12, 2003 article in *The New Yorker* by Seymour M. Hersh, in the days after September 11, Wolfowitz created the Pentagon's Office of Special Plans.[258] By the fall of 2002, "the operation rivaled both the C.I.A. and the Pentagon's own Defense Intelligence Agency, the D.I.A., as President Bush's main source of intelligence regarding Iraq's possible possession of weapons of mass destruction and connection with Al Qaeda."[259] Hersh reported that those in the Pentagon's Office of Special Plans "call themselves, self-mockingly, the Cabal."[260]

It now appears that this operation cooked the books. Hersh quoted one intelligence official who has since left the Bush administration:

> One of the reasons I left was my sense that they were using the intelligence from the C.I.A. and other agencies only when it fit their agenda. They didn't like the intelligence they were getting, and so they brought in people to write the stuff. They were so crazed and so far out and so difficult to reason with— to the point of being bizarre. Dogmatic, as if they were on a

mission from God . . . If it doesn't fit their theory, they don't want to accept it.[261]

Former Senator Bob Kerrey, who served on the Senate Intelligence Committee, told Hersh that the Bush administration's emphasis on the national security threat posed by Iraq "was the weakest and most misleading argument we could use."[262] "It appears that they have the intelligence," Kerrey added. "The problem is, they didn't like the conclusions."[263] Or, as one senior congressional aide says, "Some are astute enough to recognize that the alleged imminent W.M.D. [weapons of mass destruction] threat to the U.S. was a pretext."[264] A pretext for regime change in Iraq and for seizing control of the Persian Gulf region.

The war against Iraq marked the Bush administration's first phase of implementing its new preemptive war doctrine. But other countries are on the President's list, including Iran, Syria, North Korea, and Libya.[265] Wolfowitz and his cabal are now firmly in control.

Within days after President Bush launched his invasion of Iraq, the *Los Angeles Times* published a piece by Arthur Schlesinger, Jr., a recognized historian and former special assistant to President John F. Kennedy. "The president," Schlesinger wrote, "has adopted a policy of 'anticipatory self-defense' that is alarmingly similar to the policy that imperial Japan employed at Pearl Harbor on a date which, as an earlier American president said it would, lives in infamy. . . . [T]oday it is we Americans who live in infamy."[266] "The Bush Doctrine," Schlesinger continued, "converts us into the world's judge, jury, and executioner—a self-appointed status that, however

benign our motives, is bound to corrupt our leadership."[267]
And Schlesinger cited the words of President Kennedy:

> We must face the fact that the United States is neither omnipo-
> tent nor omniscient—that we are only six percent of the world's
> population—that we cannot impose our will upon the other
> ninety-four percent of mankind—that we cannot right every
> wrong or reverse each adversity—and that therefore there
> cannot be an American solution to every world problem.[268]

Faced with this radical departure from decades-old doctrines
of U.S. foreign policy, the nation is at a crossroads—and the
United States Constitution now faces perhaps its greatest test.
Will the Constitution's purpose of countering unchecked
power be fulfilled? Or will the president seize further monar-
chical powers in launching new preemptive wars against
other nations? Will the Congress assume its exclusive duty to
decide whether or not to send this nation into war? Or will it,
once again, unlawfully transfer that decision-making power
to the president? Will the federal judiciary intervene to protect and uphold the Constitution? Or will it, once again,
remain on the sidelines?

And how will we, as a people, respond? This is our Constitution. This is our document. It sets forth a series of promises by which to measure this nation. It creates a social
contract between our government and the people. It provides, at the end of the day, our most important safeguard
against the rule of any tyrant or would-be king.

It is time to hold up the Constitution to the faces of those
who dare to defy it. It is time to demand our country back.

Appendix One
If I Go Down, It's Not for Something I Believed In

The following is an email exchange between two of the plaintiffs in John Doe I, et al. v. George W. Bush, et al., *on the eve of the Iraq war. One of the plaintiffs is a United States Marine who was stationed in the Persian Gulf. The other is his father. Both kept their identities protected in the case.*

Monday, March 17, 2003
Subject: Monday night

Son,

I am so sorry about the speech Bush has just given to the nation. I believe by now you are aware of the forty-eight hour ultimatum that has been given. It makes me so sad and angry to see that this government has so unjustly decided to put the lives of all you brave soldiers in harm's way for what could easily have been worked out in a peaceful manner. Know that my heart and soul will be with you at all times no matter what. I have total faith in you and know that your decisions and actions will be from the heart. It is time for you also to have total faith in yourself and what you are capable of doing. Know that thousands of prayers and good thoughts are being sent your way daily and hourly. Not only by us your family and friends, but by thousands of people around the world. We pray for your safety, for the safety of all the soldiers, and for the safety of all the people in Iraq. Know that we are here and don't worry for a second about us. We just ask that you take care of yourself, so that you will be joined again soon in better days. I am here and will take good care of your mom as she awaits your return. I love you with all my heart and soul. I send you all the blessings of your father who will be here peacefully fighting for your safe return. Be safe, listen to your heart, breathe ... and feel the love that is going your way.

Love,
Dad

Warrior-King

Tuesday, March 18, 2003
Subject: RE: Monday night

Well guys, here we go. We just launched eight of our helos to advanced bases on the border of Iraq. I was left behind only to be told to be ready at a moment's notice to pack up and leave. This is going to be a war. There is no way around it now. The decision is out of our hands, and now God only knows what is going to happen. It was really weird and emotional saying goodbye to all my fellow Marines today. I can't even think of what is going through their heads. Anyone who says they aren't scared is wrong. I don't know if it is just the waiting that is killing me or the thoughts of how many lives we are going to lose over this. My spirits are high and I know I will be OK. War is ugly and I wish there was another way around this. Now, if you don't hear from me now, it's either I went landside or they cut all communications on the boat. It's bad enough not being able to be with the people you love, but no contact at all is going to be hard. If I go down, it's not for something I believed in. All this glory and medals mean nothing. The only thing I am going to get out of this is to be grateful. I owe you guys both a lot and I am so glad to have you as my parents. I love you and always will.

Your loving son,

Appendix Two
John Doe et al. v. George W. Bush et al.
Federal District Court Transcript*

1   UNITED STATES DISTRICT COURT

2   FOR THE DISTRICT OF MASSACHUSETTS

3 - - - - - - - - - - - - - - - - - - -

4 JOHN CHRIS DOE, ET AL,

Plaintiffs

5

6   vs.   No. 03-CV-10284

7 GEORGE W. BUSH, PRESIDENT, Et Al,

Defendants

8 - - - - - - - - - - - - - - - - - - -

9   BEFORE THE HONORABLE JOSEPH L. TAURO

10   UNITED STATES DISTRICT COURT JUDGE

11   John J. Moakley U.S. Courthouse

Courtroom 20, Boston, MA

12

13 APPEARANCES:

14 For the Plaintiffs:

15

16 John C. Bonifaz, Esquire, Cristobal Bonifaz, Esquire, Law

Offices of Cristobal Bonifaz, 9 Revere Street, Jamaica Plain,

17 MA 02130

18 Jonathan Shapiro, Esquire, Stern, Shapiro, Weissberg &

Garin, 90 Canal Street, Boston, MA 02114

*Typographical errors which appear in this transcript as printed appear in the
original version provided by the court stenographer.

19

20 For the Defendants:

21 Joseph Hunt, Esquire, Matthew Lepore, Esquire, Gregory
   Katsas, Esquire, United States Department of Justice, Civil

22 Division, P.O. Box 883, Washington, D.C. 20044

23

24 Official Court Reporter: Janet M. Konarski, RMR, CRR
                           John J. Moakley U.S. Courthouse

25   1 Courthouse Way, Suite 3204
                           Boston, MA 02210

2

1 (The following hearing was held in open court before the

2 Honorable Joseph L. Tauro, United States District Judge,

3 United States District Court, District of Massachusetts, at

4 the United States Courthouse, 1 Courthouse Way, Boston,

5 Massachusetts, on February 24, 2003, commencing at 10:00 a.m.)

6   THE CLERK: Docket No. 03-10284. John Doe, Et Al,

7 versus President George W. Bush, Et Al.

8   THE COURT: Sit down everybody. Good morning.

9   THE CLERK: Counsel please identify themselves for

10 the record.

11   MR. BONIFAZ: Good morning, your Honor, my name is

12 John Bonifaz. I am the plaintiff's co-counsel. With me at

13 counsel table is Cristobal Bonifaz and Jonathan Shapiro.

14   THE COURT: Nice to see you.

15   MR. HUNT: Good morning, your Honor. I'm Joseph

16 Hunt, Counsel for the United States. With me today are

17 Mr. Gregory Katsas and Mr. Matthew Lepore from the Department

18 of Justice and Bunker Henderson from the U.S. Attorneys

19 Office.

20   THE COURT: Nice to see everybody. As the first item

21 of business, I have the motion to add some parties. I take it

22 there is no objection to that?

23   MR. HUNT: We have no objection.

24   THE COURT: Okay. So, we'll allow that, and

25 hopefully everything else will run as smoothly, and it will be

3

1 a very interesting morning.

2   I have read your papers carefully and feel that I

3 understand your respective positions. You don't have to

4 repeat everything that is in the papers. On the other hand,

5 feel free to take as much time as you want to get your points

6 across, anything that you want to highlight for me, don't feel

7 that there is any time limit on it, so any time you're ready,

8 go ahead.

9   MR. BONIFAZ: Thank you, your Honor. May it please

10 the Court, my name is John Bonifaz. I'm co-counsel for the

11 plaintiffs. Your Honor, at the heart of this case is the

12 fundamental question: Who decides whether or not to send this

13 nation into war?

14   The government has made an extraordinary claim

15 that the President has unilateral authority, unilateral

16 authority under the Constitution to commence a premeditated,

17 preemptive invasion of Iraq before any attack on the United

18 States, its citizens or military, or any of its allies has

19 occurred. There is no precedent for such an exercise of

20 presidential power.

21   Article One, Section 8 of the United States

22 Constitution makes clear that Congress and only Congress has

23 the power to declare war. Your Honor, Congress has not

24 declared war or taken any equivalent action. The plaintiffs,

25 who are U.S. soldiers, parents of U.S. soldiers and members of

4

1 Congress, are before this Court today seeking judicial

2 intervention to uphold the constitution and to ensure that the

3 momentous decision of whether thousands of American soldiers

4 are to be sent into harm's way will be made by the elected

5 body of the United States Congress.

6   The plaintiffs, your Honor, satisfy the

7 requirement for a preliminary injunction. First, they are

8 likely to succeed on the merits.

9   THE COURT: Excuse me. Would you like, would you be

10 more comfortable using the podium?

11   MR. BONIFAZ: No. I'm okay right here. Thank you.

12   THE COURT: Okay.

13   MR. BONIFAZ: They are likely to succeed on the

14 merits of their claims. First, the President lacks

15 constitutional authority to commence war absent a

16 Congressional declaration of war. This is quite clear.

17   THE COURT: Of course, he hasn't commenced war.

18   MR. BONIFAZ: He has not commenced war, but war is

19 imminent by his own words and the words of the defense

20 secretary. We are —

21   THE COURT: Do we know whether those words are

22 anything more than a tactical exercise by him in an effort to

23 try to avoid war? I mean do we know that? Can I know that?

24   MR. BONIFAZ: We believe, your Honor, this Court can

25 take judicial notice of public statements that have been made

5

1 that this administration is weeks, if not days before

2 initiating an invasion of Iraq, and that those statements —

3 THE COURT: I guess my point is can I know that that

4 is anything more than, and I'm not being dismissive when I say

5 this, anything more than tough talk designed to perhaps avoid

6 a war? Can I know that?

7 MR. BONIFAZ: Your Honor, the question goes certainly

8 to ripeness, and Dellums v. Bush did address this question of

9 ripeness. That was the case brought before the first Persian

10 Gulf War. There is a difference between this and that case.

11 First, here we have a situation where there are in

12 fact already special operations troops in Iraq. Washington

13 Post article, February 13, the day of the filing of this case,

14 said, "U.S. special operations troops are already operating in

15 various parts of Iraq. They are laying the groundwork for

16 conventional U.S. forces that could quickly seize large

17 portions of Iraq if President Bush gives a formal order to go

18 to war", the official said.

19 It is not his decision to make as to whether or

20 not to send troops into war. It is a decision of the United

21 States Congress, and this Court can take judicial notice that

22 that is about to occur and that the irreparable harm that is

23 about to be inflicted upon the plaintiff soldiers in this case

24 and the other plaintiffs satisfies that prong of preliminary

25 injunction requirement, but back to the likelihood of success

6

1 of the merits, the only, the only thing that the defendants

2 can point to that has any claim of an equivalent action is the

3 October resolution passed last October by the United States

4 Congress, and that resolution, your Honor, delegated a

5 non-delegable power to the President. It delegated to the

6 President the power of whether or not to decide. It said to

7 him that he could make the determination of whether or not

8 this country launches a wholesale invasion of Iraq, an

9 occupation of that country, a regime change, something on the

10 scale that, nothing that has been seen before in the United

11 States history, this kind of preemptive, premeditated

12 invasion.

13   That October resolution cannot be seen as a

14 declaration of war or equivalent action satisfying

15 Article One, Section 8 requirements. Congress can no more

16 have seated the power to declare war to the President than it

17 could have seated its power to levy taxes or to appropriate

18 money, and in fact in Clinton v. City of New York, which the

19 United States Supreme Court decided in 1998, the Court

20 specifically dealt with this kind of transference of

21 Congressional power to the President, which could not satisfy

22 the constitutional mandate.

23   In that case, it was the line item veto act, and

24 the majority found it violated the presentment clause of the

25 U.S. Constitution.

7

1   THE COURT: But, whatever your argument, whatever the

2 merits of your argument may be with respect to whether that

3 October resolution is an overreach in terms of extending

4 power, can't it be argued that for the purposes of determining

5 jurisdiction, the October resolution indicates there is no

6 resolute conflict between the President and the legislature?

7   I note from reading your briefs you're very much

8 aware that that is a particularly important issue in

9 determining whether I have any jurisdiction at all. So, you

10 can get to that now or sometime during the course of your
11 argument.

12   MR. BONIFAZ: Yes, your Honor. We're well aware that
13 is in fact a standard some courts, including this very Court
14 articulated in Drinan v. Nixon. We have two responses.

15   First, we don't, with all due respect, believe
16 that Congressional silence in the face of a President's march
17 towards war satisfies Article One, Section 8 requirements;
18 that is to say, that that conflict is a standard that doesn't
19 meet the test in Dellums v. Bush or Orlando v. Laird. So,
20 there are courts that are divided on this, but with respect to
21 the conflict point in this particular case, there is a clear
22 conflict in our alternative reading of the October resolution,
23 which is the October resolution, at best, at best, gave the
24 President the authority to go to war only with UN approval,
25 and that resolution has very clear language on this point.

8

1 Both sections dealing under the title Authorization For Use Of
2 The United States Armed Forces state this. The President is
3 authorized to use the armed forces of the United States as he
4 determines to be necessary, that delegation point, and
5 appropriate in order to, one, defend the national security of
6 the United States against the continuing threat opposed by
7 Iraq, and, and, your Honor, enforce all relevant United
8 Nations Security Council resolutions regarding Iraq. It
9 wasn't or. It was "and".

10   In fact, the legislative history behind the
11 October resolution demonstrates many members of Congress voted
12 for this resolution with that in mind, that the President's
13 arm—hand, rather, would be strengthened going back to the

14 United Nations to reinitiate the inspections process and that
15 this UN approval was a condition before the President goes to
16 war.

17   Here we have a situation where the President is
18 saying that, one, he'll decide, as if it's his decision to
19 make, but, second, that he will do it regardless of whether or
20 not he has UN approval. The country will go it alone, if
21 necessary.

22   That is not what Congress intended. That is not
23 what Congress stated in the October resolution. The House in
24 international committee relations report also highlights this
25 point, and we have stated it in our brief, and they quoted his

9

1 speech, in which they said, "President Bush committed the
2 United States to work with the United Nations Security Council
3 and to work for the necessary resolutions", and, further, as
4 we stated in Footnote 3 of our reply brief, there were members
5 of Congress who spoke to this on the floor of the House and
6 Senate with respect to this debate.

7   Representative Tom Allen of Maine said this very
8 clearly, when he said, "The resolution authorizes the use of
9 force today through the United Nations, but it provides no
10 blank check now for unilateral military action." This was the
11 clear intent, and that is the conflict that this Court now
12 faces, a conflict between Congressional authority in this
13 alternative reading, to go to war only with UN approval, and
14 an Executive Branch's determination to go to war without it.

15   So, that conflict brings us to the political
16 question point, which is, of course, what your Honor was
17 asking, and this is a matter that is fit for judicial review.

18 As in Dellums, this Article One, Section 8 requirement cannot

19 be read out of the Constitution, as the Court found in

20 Dellums, and in Orlando v. Laird, as well. There are judicial

21 manageable standards for reviewing this kind of critical

22 question, momentous decision for the nation.

23   That is what we are asking this Court to do, to

24 read this resolution, interpret it for what it says, and see

25 that this conflict exists, requiring this intervention. With

10

1 respect to irreparable harm, your Honor, it is clear that this

2 harm is actual, and it's imminent. The plaintiff soldiers

3 face possible death or—

4   THE COURT: Where, what do you say about the resolute

5 conflict?

6   MR. BONIFAZ: The resolute conflict—

7   THE COURT: Doesn't there have to be resolute

8 conflict before the Court has jurisdiction? Otherwise, it's a

9 political question.

10   MR. BONIFAZ: Again, your Honor, our view is

11 Congressional silence does not suffice, but if you were to

12 find—

13   THE COURT: Well—

14   MR. BONIFAZ: —conflict exists—

15   THE COURT: I don't mean to interrupt you, but you

16 make an interpretation of that October resolution. There is

17 another one that could be made that is a little more positive

18 in terms of showing support, and the reasons for the vote by

19 various Congressmen, you know, may deal with motive, their

20 motive, but you know as well as I that a Congressman's motive

21 in voting is not what's key. It's the impact of the vote and

22 what the vote actually says, and my question to you is don't

23 we need to have an appearance of resolute conflict between the

24 branches in order for the judicial power to kick in?

25   That is the simple question.

11

1   MR. BONIFAZ: Right. Again, your Honor, we don't

2 believe that that conflict is necessary in order for

3 Article One, Section 8 requirements to be upheld.

4 Congressional silence does not suffice.

5   THE COURT: I'm not talking about Congressional

6 silence. I might agree with Congressional silence doesn't

7 suffice, but there has to be some indication of disagreement.

8 I think you make a good point, silence is not the—not

9 deciding.

10   MR. BONIFAZ: Right.

11   THE COURT: But, I think you make a good point. I'm

12 willing to go down that trail with you, but here don't we have

13 more than silence?

14   MR. BONIFAZ: Fair enough, your Honor, but I think

15 the point here is that if we were to even read that other

16 interpretation that the government wants us to read, that

17 somehow this was an "or" situation, not "and" situation, at

18 best that demonstrates that the resolution is ambiguous,

19 because one section it uses "and", one section it uses "or",

20 so in order to then determine what was the intent, we have to

21 go to the legislative history, in the first place, and we have

22 to go to the House report, the committee report that put

23 forward this resolution, those who drafted it. And there,

24 they say in their report, the House International Relations

25 Committee concluded that the resolution should permit use of

12

1 the military force in Iraq only "under certain circumstances".

2 This was conditioned on certain things occurring.

3   The committee took the view providing the

4 President with the authority he needs to use forces is the

5 best way to avoid force to persuade Iraq to meet its

6 international obligations and to persuade members of the

7 Security Council and others in the international community to

8 join us in bringing pressure on Iraq. The committee also

9 limited the President's authority to actions taken in

10 accordance with the Constitution and relevant laws of the

11 United States. So, the President did not get a blank check.

12   The President did not get a blank check to do

13 whatever he wanted, no matter what the United Nations Security

14 Council said, no matter what France, China, Russia said, no

15 matter what our allies said. He did not get that blank check.

16 At best, what he got was authority to go forward under the

17 international obligations that we ourselves are imposing on

18 Iraq, and saying that we need to operate within the UN

19 structure if we're going to invade Iraq, if we're going to

20 launch this wholesale invasion of Iraq.

21   That is clear from the legislative intent, it's

22 not just members' statements on the floor of the House and

23 Senate. It's in the House report, itself. So, our position

24 again is that the President does not have a blank check, and

25 it's precisely this kind of check and balances that has been

13

1 written into the United States Constitution, with this very

2 momentous kind of decision of whether or not to send a nation

3 to war. There is the check of the United States Congress, but

4 then there is also the check of this Court, and the judiciary

5 has a role and responsibility to intervene when that kind of

6 conflict has emerged, as it has today.

7   On the irreparable harm point, these harms are

8 actual, and they are imminent. Plaintiffs John Doe 1, 2, and

9 3, are United States soldiers, who are about to be sent into

10 harm's way. They face possible death or injury as a result of

11 being forced into an illegal and unconstitutional war. And,

12 your Honor, this is a voluntary Army, as we know. We don't

13 have a draft today. These soldier plaintiffs signed up. They

14 did sign up, but they signed up to play by the rules, and that

15 meant their commander in chief had to play by the rules, too.

16   They did not sign up to play by the system of

17 unchecked power, and yet that is what they're being asked to

18 do today. John Doe 2 is a Marine stationed in the Persian

19 Gulf, who clearly, who clearly faces imminent harm, as do the

20 other plaintiff soldiers. The parents of these soldiers face

21 the imminent and actual harm of the death of their sons or

22 serious injury to their sons, psychological trauma associated

23 with the horrors of war.

24   With respect to the third prong, public interest

25 clearly will be served, your Honor, by this injunction. Time

14

1 permits, time permits for the President to go back to the

2 United States Congress and seek a declaration of war. The

3 public interest is served by ensuring that when we send this

4 nation into war, we do it according to the procedures outlined

5 in the United States Constitution that the framers intended,

6 that the elected body of the United States Congress would make

7 this decision, not one single individual heading up the

8 Executive Branch.

9   With respect to the final prong, balancing the

10 harms, again, it clearly weighs in favor of the plaintiffs.

11 Time permits, time permits. If the President is right that we

12 are days, weeks away from an invasion—

13   THE COURT: You keep saying time permits. How does

14 that stack up against the argument that the President has not

15 made any sort of irrevocable commitment to war?

16   MR. BONIFAZ: Your Honor, there are 150,000 troops on

17 the border of Iraq. The planned, preeminent, premeditated

18 invasion of Iraq is clearly in the works. Furthermore, this

19 Washington Post article I cited demonstrates that special

20 operations troops are already in Iraq, laying the groundwork

21 for massive invasion. We're talking about, from public

22 reports, thousands of missiles being launched in the first

23 week. The Korean War in one week, in terms of its intensity.

24   This is clearly at the point for this Court to

25 decide. The ripeness concern is not present, but,

15

1 furthermore, on the ripeness question, your Honor, the

2 defendants cannot have it both ways. They cannot come to this

3 Court, as they did in Dellums, and say it's not ripe and then

4 come to the Court in Connors v. Regan, which was brought after

5 the invasion of Grenada, and say it's moot.

6   If it's not ripe today, and it's moot after the

7 invasion, it will never be ripe. There will never be an

8 opportunity for the Courts to review these kinds of matters.

9 This is as ripe as it will ever be for this Court to decide,

10 and it's further down the path than the Dellums case was.

11 We've discussed the political question point.

12   On the ripeness issue, as well, our clients, our

13 soldier plaintiffs, should not have to wait until they're in a

14 foxhole dodging bullets in order to be able to bring this kind

15 of claim. This is imminent, and it's already occurring in

16 certain portions of Iraq.

17   On the standing matter, your Honor, these

18 plaintiffs clearly have standing. They satisfy the

19 three-prong test of standing. The soldier plaintiffs have

20 standing in that they face an actual concrete harm, death or

21 injury, psychological trauma associated with war.

22   Now, the defendants try to say, well, two of these

23 soldier plaintiffs are not yet in Iraq, they're still in the

24 United States. They're activated, but they're not yet over

25 there. Your Honor, they could be there in a day. They could

16

1 be there in a day. It's clear that they face this actual

2 harm, and it's also clear with all three of them that it is

3 bolt redressable by this Court and that it's these defendants

4 that are engaging in sending them into an illegal and

5 unconstitutional war, but John Doe 2 is particularly important

6 because, of course, he's already based in the Persian Gulf as

7 a United States Marine, and he has a clear standing claim.

8   Now, the defendants suggest that we need to be

9 more specific about John Doe 2, beyond the fact he's a United

10 States Marine and that he's stationed in the Persian Gulf.

11 They want his coordinates. They want to know where he is.

12   Your Honor, precisely because these are plaintiffs

13 filed under pseudonyms, it's because they fear harsh

14 retaliation were they to have their identities revealed.

15   THE COURT: You made that point in your brief. I
16 understand.

17   MR. BONIFAZ: And with respect to the parents of
18 these soldiers, they, too, have standing to bring these
19 claims. Again, the defendants cannot have it both ways. They
20 can't say that the soldier plaintiffs need to identify
21 themselves more, but that the parents don't have the ability
22 to bring these kinds of claims on behalf of their sons.

23   Finally, members of Congress have standing, your
24 Honor, because they are about to be disenfranchised of their
25 constitutional right to vote on behalf of the people they

17

1 represent, of whether or not to send this nation into war.
2 Your Honor, this is a—

3   THE COURT: Isn't that a tougher question with
4 respect to them, if you don't produce a majority of the
5 Congressmen, the proposition that you're espousing?

6   MR. BONIFAZ: It is a tougher question, but we do not
7 believe that the Raines decision is dispositive on this,
8 because it's not about diluting Congressional responsibility.
9 It's wholesale disenfranchising, but, more importantly, your
10 Honor, as this Court knows, so long as one party has standing
11 in the case, the others may remain, and that has been cited in
12 our brief.

13   Finally, your Honor, this is a critical question
14 of separation of powers, but not how the defendants would cite
15 it. It's a critical question of separation of powers to
16 ensure that this momentous decision about to be made not be
17 made by the President of the United States, but that it be

18 made by the United States Congress, as was intended by the
19 framers in drafting Article One, Section 8, and it is now this
20 Court's responsibility and duty to intervene and ensure that
21 that critical clause of the Constitution be upheld. Thank
22 you.

23   THE COURT: Okay. Thank you. Mr. Hunt? Would you
24 feel more comfortable at the little lectern? You may use it,
25 too.

18

1   MR. HUNT: Thank you. I feel fine here.
2   THE COURT: Okay. Good.
3   MR. HUNT: If it please the Court, my name is Joseph
4 Hunt. I'm counsel for the United States, here before you
5 today on behalf of the President of the United States and the
6 Secretary of Defense.

7   This is a case about the authority of the
8 President to commit United States Armed Forces to protect the
9 national security interests of the United States against the
10 threat posed by Iraq. It is an issue—

11   (Noise interference.)

12   THE COURT: Try again.

13   MR. HUNT: It is an issue, your Honor, over which
14 there is agreement between the Legislative and Executive
15 Branches. Every Court to have decided this issue, and there
16 have been a number in the past 30 years to have reached a
17 similar question, including this Court, have decided that this
18 is an issue that the Court should refrain from intervening in.

19   In Drinan v. Nixon, your Honor, this Court said
20 that this issue was a non-judicial political question. Faced
21 with the challenge brought by members of the House of

112

22 Representatives and a member of the military, this Court said

23 that the question was, and I quote, "beyond the authority of a

24 Federal Court to hear or determine," as was the case in

25 Drinan, there is no conflict. There is no disagreement here.

19

1   In fact, the Legislative Branch has spoken,

2 showing its support and ratification for the President's use

3 of force. Among other things, in the October resolution, the

4 joint resolution expressly supports the President's use of

5 American armed forces, as he deems necessary and appropriate

6 to defend the national security interests of the United States

7 and to enforce all relevant United Nations Security Council

8 resolutions regarding Iraq.

9   Now, plaintiffs would ask this Court to believe

10 that that resolution really means that the President can only

11 use his authority to commit forces if there has first been an

12 attack by Iraq, and if the United Nations Security Council

13 decides that there should be war with Iraq.

14   First, your Honor, the resolution does not say

15 that, when it clearly could have, if that is what was

16 intended. Indeed, your Honor, Plaintiff Congressmen here,

17 including Congressman Kucinich, in a 60-minute speech on the

18 floor stated that this authority of the President under this

19 resolution was so broad as to allow the President to order an

20 attack against Iraq. I quote. He says, "This language is so

21 broad that it would allow the President to order an attack

22 against Iraq." He didn't believe at the time that this

23 resolution meant that the President could only commit troops

24 if there had first been an attack by Iraq, and he didn't say

25 that it depended upon the United Nations first making a

1 determination of the propriety of getting involved in a war

2 with Iraq.

3   The plain language of the resolution, your Honor,

4 moreover, states that the President may determine, as he

5 determines necessary and appropriate, whether or not it's

6 necessary to enforce the United Nations Security Council

7 resolutions. It doesn't say first the Security Council must

8 act.

9   Finally, as we point out in our brief, the very

10 next section says that once the President has committed the

11 armed forces of the United States, he is to report to the

12 Congress that diplomatic means were unavailable at that point,

13 either to protect the national security interests of the

14 United States or to enforce the United Nations Security

15 Council resolutions. Failing to persuade their colleagues in

16 the Congress that they shouldn't pass this joint resolution,

17 the Plaintiff Congressmen here now ask this Court to get

18 involved.

19   Plaintiffs would have this Court believe, your

20 Honor, that the joint resolution is an unconstitutional

21 abdication of Congress's power under the Constitution to

22 declare war, but nothing stops Congress now or any time from

23 voting on whether or not to declare war.

24   In Massachusetts v. Laird, your Honor, this

25 circuit, and I note that plaintiffs have not one time

1 addressed the question or the precedent of Massachusetts v.

2 Laird, binding in this jurisdiction on a relevant question

3 that they've raised before this Court. In Massachusetts v.

4 Laird, the Court, the circuit said, "Where the Executive

5 continues to act not only in the absence of any conflicting

6 Congressional claim of authority, but with steady

7 Congressional support, the Constitution has not been

8 breached."

9 Applying that principle, your Honor, this Court in

10 Drinan, said, "Given a challenge to the constitutionality of

11 an undeclared military operation, the Court's role is to

12 determine whether in some manner Congress has expressly or

13 impliedly ratified his actions.

14 As this circuit noted in Massachusetts v. Laird,

15 your Honor, the Constitution does not say that, and the

16 framers when they framed the Constitution did not say no war

17 shall be engaged in without a declaration by Congress. While

18 the Court need look no further than the First Circuit's

19 decision in Massachusetts v. Laird, and its own decision in

20 Drinan v. Nixon, there are numerous cases cited in our brief,

21 your Honor, in which Courts have, for one reason or another,

22 on justiciability grounds determined this was an issue in

23 which the Court should not get involved.

24 The Court in Ange v. Bush, your Honor, prior to

25 Operation Desert Storm and I might add in instances where

22

1 special operations forces had been at work there, as well,

2 prior to Operation Desert Storm, the Court there said, and I

3 quote, because I think it encapsulates very well why the

4 political question doctrine precludes the Court from

5 intervening in a situation like this. The Court in Ange said,

6 "The judgments required for war powers purposes are delicate,

7 complex, and involve elements of prophecy. They are and
8 should be undertaken only by those directly responsible to the
9 people, whose welfare they advance or imperil. They are
10 decisions of a kind for which the judiciary has neither the
11 aptitude, facilities nor responsibility and which has long
12 been held to belong in the domain of political power, not
13 subject to judicial intrusion or inquiry."

14   The overwhelming weight of authority, your Honor,
15 is that in questions such as these, the political question
16 doctrine, as formulated by the Supreme Court in Baker v. Carr,
17 precludes judicial intervention to make determinations that it
18 does not have the facilities to make. There are no measurable
19 standards, your Honor, by which the Court must undertake
20 questions that are directly relevant to the decisions related
21 to war.

22   The war powers are textually committed to the
23 Legislative and Executive Branches. For those reasons, for
24 the reasons of a lack of respect due to the coordinate
25 branches were the judiciary to become involved, the Supreme

23

1 Court has said in Baker v. Carr that they should not, and
2 indeed as I pointed out every Court has for one reason or
3 another, largely with respect to political question,
4 determined that it should not.

5   I will briefly, your Honor, just touch about upon
6 the questions of standing and ripeness. We rely on what we
7 stated in our briefs, your Honor, with respect to those
8 issues. We think it clear that under Raines these Plaintiff
9 Congressmen do not have standing before this Court.

10   Indeed, just as plaintiffs here have tried to do

11 and come within what they regard as the Coleman exception to
12 Raines, that was tried in the Campbell case, a case in which
13 Congressmen went to Court to block the President's use of
14 force with respect to Kosovo. There the Court said under
15 Raines, Plaintiff Congressmen have no constitutional power to
16 challenge the President's war making authorities in Federal
17 Court.

18   Your Honor, with respect to the John Doe
19 plaintiffs, as we point out in our brief, and in particular
20 John Doe 2, while he's stationed in the Persian Gulf, we do
21 not know enough, the plaintiffs have not provided this Court
22 with enough, particularly for purposes of a preliminary
23 injunction, on whether or not he is there for purposes of a
24 war with Iraq. We don't know whether based on what the
25 plaintiffs have told the Court that he may be there to protect

24

1 American embassies in the Persian Gulf, whether he may be
2 there for the ongoing war against terrorism, or whether he may
3 be there for some reason wholly unrelated to planned military
4 activities vis-a-vis Iraq.

5   With respect to the other John Doe plaintiffs, one
6 of them we know has not even been activated, but is merely
7 expecting to be called into activated duly. The other one has
8 been activated, but has not yet even gotten orders to report
9 to the Persian Gulf.

10   With respect, your Honor, to the question of
11 ripeness, nobody, your Honor, in this courtroom knows whether
12 or not the President of the United States will commit United
13 States Armed Forces to an attack, a military attack against
14 Iraq. For months, the United States has endeavored to work on

15 a diplomatic resolution to the threat posed by Iraq, and there

16 remains the hope of a peaceful resolution. It cannot be said

17 that anyone here knows, even with, as your Honor called it,

18 the tough talk, and the tough rhetoric on this issue, that

19 that doesn't have or serve some purpose that would result in a

20 peaceful resolution of this dispute.

21   Indeed, I believe it was the Court in Ange that

22 also made a point of that, that notwithstanding the fact that

23 prior to the invasion in Operation Desert Storm, that it was

24 unclear even weeks before that whether or not the United

25 States would ultimately commit troops vis-a-vis Iraq.

25

1   In such circumstances, your Honor, it would be

2 premature for this Court to step in and exercise its judgment

3 on the matter when the Constitution has clearly committed this

4 authority to the President of the United States. And on that

5 point, your Honor, even if we were to get beyond the

6 justiciability questions, and we don't understand, your Honor,

7 how it could be possible in these circumstances where there is

8 agreement between the Legislative and Executive Branches on

9 this question, even if we were to reach the merits here, your

10 Honor, the Constitution is clear that the President of the

11 United States has full executive power, and that the

12 President, as commander in chief, has the authority to commit

13 troops to protect the national security interests of the

14 United States.

15   The Constitution doesn't say that the President

16 must first wait for Congress to declare war. Congress

17 unquestionably, to be sure, has the power to declare war, but

18 no Court has ever held that that is a prerequisite to the

19 President's use of force, and in fact history demonstrates

20 that most, on most occasions the Executive has used its

21 constitutional authority to engage United States Armed Forces

22 without a declaration of war.

23   If the Court has no questions, I would end, your

24 Honor, with simply this thought: It is quite clear that were

25 the President to undertake military operations in Iraq, he

26

1 would be acting pursuant to the Constitution, pursuant to the

2 Supreme Court precedent that has recognized the President's

3 authority to engage United States Armed Forces in hostilities,

4 pursuant to the precedent of this circuit, and indeed of this

5 very Court, and pursuant to a history of Executive and

6 Legislative Branch practice, and, very importantly, here,

7 pursuant to the express approval of Congress by means of a

8 joint resolution.

9   This Court in Drinan said it would not second

10 guess the method by which Congress chooses to demonstrate its

11 support and ratification for the President's use of force.

12 Here, the Congress has done so by means of the joint

13 resolution. The President's power under these circumstances,

14 your Honor, is in the oft quoted words of Justice Jackson in

15 the Youngstown Steel case, at its apex, because the President

16 is not only undertaking his authority granted him by the

17 Constitution, but everything that Congress could delegate in

18 that regard.

19   The plaintiffs' attempt here, your Honor, to

20 challenge the President's authority is unwarranted, and this

21 case should be dismissed. They have failed to meet the

22 standards for preliminary injunction for all the reasons that

23 I've noted with respect to justiciability. They do not stand

24 a likelihood of success on the merits, your Honor, and we ask

25 this Court to deny their motion for preliminary injunction and

27

1 to dismiss their action.

2   THE COURT: Do you want to be heard some more?

3   MR. BONIFAZ: Yes, your Honor. Thank you. Just a

4 few points in response. First, with respect to the

5 defendant's questions raised by John Doe 2 or even the other

6 John Does, your Honor, we're prepared to present to you the

7 identities en camera, ex parte, but we're just not prepared to

8 share that information with the government, but we're

9 certainly prepared to demonstrate to you these are real

10 individuals, and they're in the United States Armed Forces.

11   With respect to the questions raised by

12 Massachusetts v. Laird and most of the other cases that the

13 defendants site, there is a critical distinction between those

14 cases, your Honor, including Dinan v. Nixon and this. We're

15 not in the middle or even toward the end of a war, as those

16 cases were. We're at the very initiation of it, so there is

17 not this concurrent authority shared by the commander in

18 chief.

19   THE COURT: Why does that make a difference?

20   MR. BONIFAZ: It makes a difference.

21   THE COURT: Help me out on that.

22   MR. BONIFAZ: It makes a difference, because once war

23 has begun, then there are shared powers between a President,

24 as commander in chief, and the Congress, but this is much more

25 like Dellums v. Bush, in which the Court found it was not a

28

1 political question prior to the initiation of Persian Gulf

2 War 1, and the Court could review this matter. I would also

3 turn the Court's attention to Judge Tatel's concurring

4 opinion.

5 THE COURT: On the political question issue, if the

6 Congress, let's say, had clearly stated no war in Iraq,

7 unanimous vote, if that could ever be possible in both

8 branches, and the President said, I am not bound by that, now

9 you have resolute conflict, at least more resolute conflict.

10 Yet, no war had started yet. So, I just don't understand the

11 significance of the fact that there may be a war in action,

12 you know, there may be a war in fact, how that affects whether

13 or not there is a resolute opposition between parties.

14 MR. BONIFAZ: Because, as your Honor found in Drinan

15 v. Nixon, there was Congressional participation in the

16 decision making and in prosecuting that war. There were

17 military appropriations that had taken place. There was a

18 draft and repeated extensions of the draft.

19 THE COURT: I understand. It isn't whether the war

20 started or not that is determinative of the political question

21 issue.

22 MR. BONIFAZ: Well, I take your point, your Honor,

23 but the point I'm making here is that once war starts there is

24 a whole lot of other things that Congress can begin to do,

25 including financing the operations.

29

1 THE COURT: I understand.

2 MR. BONIFAZ: Draft, that did not occur, has not

3 occurred here, and was the case in Massachusetts v. Laird and
4 nearly all of the other cases that the defendants cite, but
5 further, again, your Honor, the war has started, as I've
6 identified here, with special operations troops already in
7 Iraq, and so the President in many ways has already initiated
8 this without Congressional approval.
9   The defendants cite Baker v. Carr, but Baker v.
10 Carr does not stand for the principle that political cases
11 raise political questions. It is not the case that because
12 this raises matters that are also political in nature that it
13 necessarily is a political question. What is at stake here —
14   THE COURT: No, but Baker v. Carr recognizes the fact
15 that certain branches have certain prerogatives. That is
16 the—
17   MR. BONIFAZ: Yes.
18   THE COURT: If you trespass on the prerogative, that
19 is where you run the risk of political question.
20   MR. BONIFAZ: Absolutely, your Honor, but in the
21 final analysis, the majority in that decision found that it
22 was their duty as a court to interpret the Constitution and
23 uphold and that nothing less could they do then to ensure the
24 Constitution would be upheld, so they have been warned, they
25 have been warned not to go into that political thicket of the

30

1 redistricting matters. They have been warned to stay away
2 from it, and the State Supreme Court of Tennessee in the
3 previous Baker v. Carr, before it went to the Supreme Court,
4 itself, had stated that the destruction of the State of
5 Tennessee could occur if there were court intervention.
6 Clearly, Tennessee was not destroyed. It still stands, and it

7 survive the Supreme Court ruling of Baker v. Carr, the one

8 person, one vote principle is now the law of the land.

9   It was critically important for that court to

10 intervene, as it is here. The defendants cite Youngstown for

11 this proposition, but we don't see how Youngstown supports

12 them. Youngstown was an example of sweeping presidential

13 power that had to be checked, and the Court stepped in and

14 ensured that the seizure of those steel mills was not within

15 the constitutional power of the President.

16   Again, the defendant's claims there may be a

17 peaceful resolution—

18   THE COURT: There was no political issue. There was

19 politics, but there was no political issue, in that, as I

20 recall the case, there wasn't any manifest intent on the part

21 of the Congress to disagree with the President's seizure.

22 Have I got that wrong?

23   MR. BONIFAZ: In Youngstown?

24   THE COURT: Yes.

25   MR. BONIFAZ: The point of that decision was there

31

1 was no authority that the President had to seize these mills,

2 and it was—

3   THE COURT: Silence.

4   MR. BONIFAZ: Exactly.

5   THE COURT: You talked about silence.

6   MR. BONIFAZ: Exactly. And then with respect to

7 this, again, this point that somehow that we can wait,

8 basically, is a claimed defense we're making, we can still

9 wait. Your Honor, if we can wait, that means essentially we

10   need to wait until bombs start falling until we go into this

11 Court, and then the harm, the irreparable harm will clearly
12 have already occurred. And, again, they're already there.
13 Special operations troops are already inside Iraq, laying the
14 groundwork for an invasion.

15   Finally, your Honor, the defendants make this
16 incredible, extraordinary sweeping claim that there is
17 unilateral executive power to engage in this premeditated,
18 preemptive invasion of an entire country, an occupation of
19 that country, regime change. This is nothing, nothing like
20 anything we've seen before in the United States history.

21   They come before this Court and say the President
22 can do it alone. This is precisely, precisely what the
23 framers intended would not happen when they put Article One,
24 Section 8 in the United States Constitution, to ensure that
25 the Presidents of these United States would not be like

32

1 European monarchs of the past. There are two critical
2 distinctions, critical distinctions among many, but the two
3 most critical between this country and the founding of it, and
4 those European monarchs of the past, one is regarding popular
5 elections, and the other is regarding that momentous decision
6 of whether or not to send a nation to war.

7   It is not about one person, who sends his subjects
8 off into battle. It is about the elective body of the United
9 States Congress. The President does not have this kind of
10 unilateral executive power that the defendants claim he does,
11 and no Court has ever found that the President has that kind
12 of power, and the very fact that they come before this Court
13 and make that kind of sweeping claim demonstrates what is at

14 stake here. The President has been all over the country,

15 saying he will decide. He will decide whether or not we go to

16 war.

17   Your Honor, it is not his decision to make. It is

18 the decision of the United States Congress. Thank you.

19   THE COURT: Anything else?

20   MR. HUNT: Just a couple of points, your Honor.

21   THE COURT: Go ahead.

22   MR. HUNT: Your Honor, plaintiffs suggest that they

23 perhaps could present affidavits to the Court en camera with

24 respect to the John Doe plaintiffs. In that regard, I would

25 suggest we don't think the Court need to reach that because of

33

1 the threshold political question doctrine.

2   THE COURT: I understand.

3   MR. HUNT: With respect to the distinction that in

4 other circumstances we were in a period where the war had been

5 ongoing and Congress had somehow shown its ratification and

6 support, indeed, that support was found implicitly in

7 circumstances where Congress had appropriated funds.

8   Here, we have an explicit authorization in the

9 form of the House joint resolution, and indeed were Congress

10 here to still choose, it could put a bill on the floor,

11 Congress could vote and say we're not going to appropriate any

12 funds to go to war with Iraq. They still have the ability to

13 do that, just as I said before, your Honor, the President here

14 has not declared war. Congress may still exercise its

15 authority to decide whether or not it wishes to vote on a

16 declaration of war.

17   And, finally, your Honor, they endeavor to cite,

18   they do cite to the Dellums case, in an attempt to show that

19   there was found to be, this was found not to be a political

20   question. Actually, your Honor, in that case, the Court did

21   not say that in every circumstance there would not be a

22   political question. What the Court there said, it was

23   unwilling to say that the question of Executive and

24   Legislative war powers was always a political question that

25   warranted judicial non-interference.

34

1   The Court in fact stated, and I'll quote, "That is

2   not to say that assuming that the issue is factually close or

3   ambiguous or fraught with intricate technical, military and

4   diplomatic baggage, the Courts would not defer to the

5   political branches to determine whether or not hostilities

6   might qualify as war", and in fact in Dellums the Court said

7   the President is entitled to be protected from an injunctive

8   order respecting a declaration of war when there is no

9   evidence that this is what the Legislative Branch, as such, as

10   distinguished from a fraction of the Legislative Branch,

11   regards as a necessary prerequisite to military moves in the

12   Arabian Desert. In Dellums the legislature had not even made

13   any decision one way or another on whether it supported the

14   President's authority to use force.

15   Here, your Honor, we have that clearly and

16   unambiguously with regard to the joint resolution.

17   THE COURT: Anything else?

18   MR. BONIFAZ: No, your Honor.

19   THE COURT: Okay. I recognize that there are

126

20 exigencies that require me to pay close attention to this case

21 this morning, and my intention is to return here in an hour

22 and give you a decision, so I'm going to be in recess. It's

23 now ten minutes of 11, so I'll be back at ten minutes of 12.

24   I'll look for you then, and I will give you my

25 decision. Okay?

35

1   THE CLERK: All rise for the Honorable Court.

2   (A recess was taken.)

3   THE CLERK: All rise for the Honorable Court.

4   THE COURT: Please be seated. Good morning again

5 everybody. Before I give my decision, I want to put on the

6 record my impression as to what an outstanding and very

7 professional job both sets of counsel have done in this case,

8 both in the written submissions and the oral argument. You're

9 to be commended.

10   Unfortunately, this isn't the kind of case I can

11 settle, so one side wins, and one side doesn't, but I guess

12 the point I want to make is with respect to counsel, there are

13 no losers here. Both sides handled yourselves in a very

14 professional way.

15   So, let me give you my conclusions here. It will

16 take just a few minutes. The plaintiffs seek to enjoin the

17 President from launching a military invasion of Iraq,

18 asserting that Congress has neither declared war, nor taken

19 any action that would give the President the power to wage

20 such a war. The defendants oppose such an injunction for

21 several reasons, including that the plaintiffs' complaint does

22 not set forth a justiciable issue, and, therefore, this Court

23 has no jurisdiction to act. The threshold issue before the
24 Court, therefore, is whether plaintiffs' complaint presents a
25 non-justiciable political question, and, therefore, must be

36

1 dismissed.
2   For the reasons I will now outline, this Court
3 concludes that the issues raised by the plaintiffs involve
4 political questions in the legal sense of that term, which are
5 beyond the authority of a Federal Court to resolve.
6   As a general proposition, the conduct of this
7 country's foreign relations involve political issues that the
8 Constitution commits for resolution to the political branches
9 of government, the Executive and the Legislative. Absent a
10 clear abdication of this constitutional responsibility by the
11 political branches, the judiciary has no role to play. For
12 example, should it become apparent that the political
13 branches, themselves, are clearly and resolutely in opposition
14 as to the military policy to be followed by the United States,
15 then the situation would have gone beyond that of the
16 political question and would pose a serious constitutional
17 issue requiring resolution by the judicial branch. So, a
18 Federal Court may judge the war policies of the political
19 branches only when the actions taken by the Congress and those
20 taken by the executive manifest clear resolute conflict
21 between them.
22   Each of the political branches has
23 responsibilities and prerogatives with respect to war policy.
24 For example, the Constitution grants to the Congress the power
25 to declare war, to raise and support armies, and to provide

1 and maintain a Navy. The President is made the commander in
2 chief of the armed forces.

3   Case law makes clear that the Congress does not
4 have the exclusive right to determine whether or not the
5 United States will engage in war. Congressional ratification
6 for the continuation of undeclared war activity may be found,
7 even though there has not been a formal declaration of
8 approval. The manner and form of ratification is up to
9 Congress, and the Courts have no power to second guess the
10 wisdom or form of such approval. The fact that Congress and
11 the President may appear to be at odds from day to day
12 concerning the conduct of military affairs doesn't necessarily
13 add up to resolute conflict between the political branches.
14

15   Dispute, debate and disagreement are the
16 prerogatives of the political branches. The controlling issue
17 for determining this Court's jurisdiction, therefore, is
18 whether such dispute and disagreement has reached a point of
19 clear and resolute conflict that would warrant judicial
20 intervention. Relevant to that inquiry in this case is the
21 Congressional October resolution concerning Iraq. Plaintiffs
22 argue that the October resolution cannot be interpreted as
23 Congressional action giving the President the power to make
24 war with Iraq. But, whatever the merits of that argument, it
25 is clear that Congress has not acted to bind the President

1 with respect to possible military activity in Iraq. And,
2 indeed, the President for his part has not irrevocably

3 committed our armed forces to military conflict in Iraq.

4 There is, therefore, a day-to-day fluidity in the situation

5 that does not amount to resolute conflict between the

6 branches, but that does argue against uninformed judicial

7 intervention.

8   Now, this memorandum I'm reciting is consistent

9 with this Court's opinion thirty years ago in the case of Drinan

10 vs. Nixon, which was cited with approval by the Second Circuit

11 in the case of Holtzman vs. Schlesinger.

12   Just formally I will state for the record

13 plaintiffs' request for injunctive relief is denied.

14 Defendant's motion to dismiss is allowed, and this memorandum

15 will be attached to the order issued today. A formal opinion,

16 further memorializing that order will issue sometime in the

17 future, but the posture of the case now will be that there was

18 an order, there is a memorandum accompanying the order, and so

19 the case is ripe for appeal, if that is the wish of the

20 plaintiffs to do so. You can do it any time, I would say from

21 five minutes, five minutes from now until I think it's ten

22 days I think you have to file a notice of appeal.

23   Okay. Do you have any questions, anything like

24 that? Again, thank you very much for a terrific job. Very

25 professional.

39

1   MR. BONIFAZ: Thank you, your Honor.

2   THE CLERK: All rise for the Honorable Court.

3   THE COURT: Zita will have copies for you, and for

4 the press if there is some interest in the text of what I just

5 had to say.

6   THE CLERK: Court is in recess.

7   (Proceedings adjourned at 11:58 a.m.)

8

9   - - - - - - - -

10   CERTIFICATION

11

12   I certify that the foregoing is a correct

13 transcript of the record of proceedings in the above-entitled

14 matter, to the best of my skill and ability.

15

16 _____   _____

       Janet M. Konarski   Date

17   Official Court Reporter

18

19

20

21

22

23

24

25

Appendix Three
John Doe et al. v. George W. Bush et al.
Federal Appellate Court Transcript*

UNITED STATES COURT OF APPEALS
FOR THE FIRST CIRCUIT

JOHN DOE, I et al.

V.   No. 03-1266

PRESIDENT GEORGE W. BUSH, et al.

ORAL ARGUMENT HELD ON MARCH 4, 2003 AT THE UNITED
STATES COURT OF APPEALS FOR THE FIRST CIRCUIT BEFORE
JUDGES SANDRA LYNCH, NORMAN STAHL, AND CONRAD CYR

APPEARANCES

John Bonifaz, Esq.

Representing Appellants John Doe I, et al.

Gregory Katsas, Esq.

Representing Appellees George W. Bush, et al.

Reporter: Raymond F. Catuogno

                            Registered Professional Reporter

                            (Transcript Prepared from Tape)

*Typographical errors which appear in this transcript as printed appear in the
original version provided by the court stenographer.

MR. BONIFAZ: Good morning, Your Honors. May it please The Court, my name is John Bonifaz, I am co-counsel for the Plaintiffs. Your Honors, imagine for a moment that Congress had passed a resolution stating the following. The President is authorized to levy an income tax on the American people as he deems necessary and appropriate in order to pay for highway construction projects. What would this court do? Would it say that it is barred from intervening to protect and uphold the Constitution? Barred from declaring such a resolution as an unconstitutional delegation of congressional power on Article I, Section 8? And barred from preventing the President from acting in such an unconstitutional manner?

JUDGE LYNCH: Mr. Bonifaz, the precise nature of the claims in front of us is something that I would like to explore with you. I think we have, if you will, two competing models somewhat contradictory that are presented in your papers. But that's okay. Lawyers present contradictory theories all the time.

The first is that there is no particular dispute between the Congress and the Executive about this issue, but that there is a dispute between your clients on the one hand and those other two branches because you say, the Constitution would not permit the Congress to enact a resolution on, and particularly a conditional resolution. I'm right, that's one of the series that you're arguing?

MR. BONIFAZ: Your Honor that is the principal theory.

JUDGE LYNCH: Are you also arguing the theory that there is a divergence of interests and some conflict between the Congress and the Executive Branch in that the Congress has expressed its views in the October Resolution, the authorization for use of military force against

Iraq and that the Executive is not in compliance with that. Is that also your argument?

MR. BONIFAZ: Yes, Your Honor, we're saying that the only way the Resolution can be read as Constitutional is if it's to be read that it requires U.N. approval. But first and foremost, we are saying that Congress did collaborate with the President an unconstitutional action.

JUDGE LYNCH: Alright. So your second argument is derivative of your first argument. So let's explore the constitutional claim. Partly it appears to be, and correct me, a magic-words argument at least in part, that because Congress did not use the term "Declaration of War," that rather used the term of "Authorization," that the Constitution does not permit Congress to do anything short of a Declaration of War. Is that your argument?

MR. BONIFAZ: No Your Honor, absolutely not. We have fully acknowledged in our briefs that Congress may declare war or take any other equivalent action to suffice its requirements under Article I, Section 8. But here what we have is nothing of the sort.

MS. LYNCH: Okay. Is the claim then that the October Resolution is not the equivalent of a Declaration? Is that it?

MR. BONIFAZ: Absolutely Your Honor. If read carefully, it is not only the words "Authorized," it says "as the President deems necessary and appropriate." It transfers to the President the decision of whether or not this nation is to be sent into war.

JUDGE LYNCH: But also requires that if the President takes certain actions, that he then report back to the Congress which presumably could then either declare a war or give further authorization or say this is contrary to our intent.

MR. BONIFAZ: Yes, but this gets strictly to the framers intent, Your Honor, which was to esure that both houses of Congress participate in a declaration of war. The constitutional default position is that we're not at war. If we're not at war in a general sense, the only way we go to war is if Congress says yes. So it cannot be that the President can take this nation into war and then Congress must then somehow say, no, we're not at war. The default position is we're not at war and before we go to war, Congress must vote. And if one house, if one house of the United States Congress votes against that, then we will not be at war. So it's not possible to go back after bombing begins.

JUDGE LYNCH: Yes, and I've read the John Hart Ely section that you rely on and I understand the argument about the political difficulties of the default position, and I assume that's part of your argument as to why the Congress needs the buttressing through the justiciability of the issues in the courts. But let's go back to why is Congress precluded from asserting conditions of the sort which are contained in the October Resolution. What is unconstitutional about an expression of Congress' power to declare war that takes this conditional form?

MR. BONIFAZ: Your Honor, again, we argue in the first instance that it did not even conditionally declare war. It transferred to the President the decision as to whether or not we're going to war. It said, as he deems it necessary. He may do this or he may not. That's not what Congress can do. It abdicated completely its responsibilities, It did so just as in the levying income tax situation.

JUDGE STAHL: If I read the Resolution in C-I, where it refers to specific authorization within the meaning of by be it the War Powers Resolution . . .

JUDGE LYNCH: Right.

JUDGE STAHL: What is your take on that? What was that supposed to mean? Isn't that an indication on the part of Congress that it was giving the President the go-ahead?

MR. BONIFAZ: It's basically saying to the President, you decide.

JUDGE STAHL: I don't think so. I think that if you read the entire Resolution and you read that particular clause, it seems to me that they're trying to go back to the original statute, the '73 Statute and to act in accordance with the requirements of that Statute.

MR. BONIFAZ: Again, Your Honor, we believe that a fair reading of this Resolution either means that it transfers unlawfully to the President the decision and this is made not just in 3-A, but 3-B the determination that the President makes, he then reports back after he's determined that we're going to war what his determination is, and then Congress gets that determination forty-eight hours after the bombing starts. That's not what the framers intended. They wanted the House of Representatives to be part of this decision not just the United States Senate. That's why they brought both chambers together on this question.

JUDGE CYR: So if we were to accept the first prong of your argument, which is to the effect that the Congress cannot simply say, you have the authority whenever you decide to exercise it . . .

MR. BONIFAZ: If . . .

JUDGE CYR: There would be in your view that can't work as long as the President doesn't act immediately.

MR. BONIFAZ: Your Honor, the issue isn't you can do it whenever you want. The issue is, if you want. That's what was done here. It wasn't, Mr. President, you can do this whenever you want. It was clear that it was, as he determines to be necessary and appropriate, he can make the decision. And do you know what? This defendant has been all over the country saying, I'll decide whether or not to send this nation to war. It's clear he understands what Congress did to him. He said that he [it] transferred the decision to him. He'll make the decision of whether we're going to war.

JUDGE CYR: But, is the decision about who is to determine whether or not as Commander-in-Chief war is indicated, as distinguished from whether or not the Congress has to say, only when it's indicated now, can Congress say you may do so.

MR. BONIFAZ: The Commander-in-Chief responsibilities do not involve declaring war, deciding whether or not to send this nation to war. The Commander-in-Chief responsibilities—even Alexander Hamilton a major proponent of executive power, stated that this was presenting a President who would be much more inferior than the kings of England. In respect to Commander-in-Chief, his role as Alexander Hamilton put it, was to be the supreme commander of the forces. That is not the same as deciding whether or not to send thousands of American soldiers into harms way. That is Congress' responsibility.

JUDGE LYNCH: Let me pose a couple of hypotheticals to you. Let's suppose that the U.N. Security Council passes a resolution that authorizes military action against Iraq, and let's assume that it's really pretty clear that one could reasonably conclude that Iraq poses a threat to the security of the United States. Are you arguing that under (1) that that would violate the October Resolution, and (2) if the October Resolution permitted it, it would be unconstitutional?

MR. BONIFAZ: The U.N. Security Council action certainly wouldn't violate the October Resolution.

JUDGE LYNCH: No, no, no. The President acting in that context.

MR. BONIFAZ: Yes, Your Honor, we're saying that the U.N. cannot trump Article I, Section 8, of our Constitution. The U.N. doesn't decide whether or not this nation should be sent into war any more than a Turkish Parliament decides whether or not Turkey should be used to put troops there.

JUDGE LYNCH: So your case really is about what you view to be the Congress' grant of conditional authority to the President to send our troops into hostile action on his determination that certain conditions exist.

MR. BONIFAZ: No, Your Honor, we don't say this is conditional declaration of war. What we say is that Congress simply transferred to the President the power to decide, and Congress could not have lawfully transferred that power, it's non-delegable power, only Congress has that power.

JUDGE STAHL: Are you saying that the War Powers Act itself is not constitutional? There's some people who think that.

JUDGE LYNCH: But they're usually on the Executive side, not on your side.

JUDGE STAHL: But I want to see what his answer to that is, because I think it's important to know that answer in light of what Congress in fact did.

MR. BONIFAZ: We don't regard the statutory authorization language, that prong in the War Powers Act, has anything but superlative to the Declaration of War requirement. It's not as if that prong can somehow trump the constitutional requirement. Insofar as it does somehow trump that requirement, then certainly it is unconstitutional. But we're not making that claim in this case.

JUDGE STAHL: Well are there any circumstances that you see where short of a declaration of war by Congress where the Executive can put troops in the field?

MR. BONIFAZ: Absolutely, Your Honor, to repel sudden attack.

JUDGE STAHL: On this country?

MR. BONIFAZ: That's right or on allies as has been interpreted by case law.

JUDGE STAHL: Well how do you get to Kosovo?

MR. BONIFAZ: Well Kosovo actually was in our view a violation. That was brought by plaintiffs who did not have any standing. But the fact is it had soldier plaintiffs been brought before the court in . . .

JUDGE STAHL: So you would have thought that the Kosovo action was equally infirmed?

MR. BONIFAZ: Absolutely, Your Honor, and the fact that prior violations have occurred doesn't change the fact this violation is about to occur. But, it's even worse than Kosovo Your Honors because this is an extraordinary situation this country has never faced before. We're facing a President who is about to launch a premeditated planned invasion of another county, the conquering of that country, the occupation of that country, not to repel sudden attack. No, because this is an Executive Branch who's determined to do this regardless of whether Congress has spoken clearly and given a Declaration of War or any equivalent action. That's not occurred in American history before.

And so this court has a duty prior to that kind of imminent and premeditated invasion of occurring of another country, first strike war, this court has a duty to interpret the constitutional actions of this President and to determine whether or not they hold up. And it's our position that they do not clearly hold up under Article I, Section 8, that this momentous decision of whether to send thousands of American soldiers into war, into battle, is a decision that must be made by the elected body of the United States Congress.

JUDGE STAHL: Let me ask you another question. Assume for the moment that the Executive had absolutely excellent information that missiles are about to be launched against the United States. Does the Executive have any first-strike capability under those circumstances?

MR. BONIFAZ: It depends on what the "about to" is. We would argue here, Your Honor, that time permits. Time permits for the President to go back to Congress. He can do it today, Congress can have an immediate debate. It isn't the same situation. The facts of this case clearly permit Congress to debate and declare whether or not we're going to war. If this were an emergency, then we would be at war already and we're not.

JUDGE LYNCH: In the second world war, wasn't there in fact an engagement before the Declaration of War was actually enacted by the Congress?

MR. BONIFAZ: There was an attack on . . .

JUDGE LYNCH: Yes, and wasn't there a response launched before there was a Declaration of War?

MR. BONIFAZ; Yes, but, again, this is . . .

JUDGE LYNCH: So the precedent is that one can already be engaged in hostilities before Congress enacts a Declaration of War?

MR. BONIFAZ: But that's not what we have here, Your Honor. Today we don't have that.

JUDGE LYNCH: Okay. Obviously I'm about to segway into ripeness.

MR. BONIFAZ: Sure, well rightness is clearly an issue that the government has raised. The government raises the issue of muteness after an invasion occurs, they did that Conyers v. Reagan. They cannot have it both ways. They cannot come before this court and say it's not ripe.

JUDGE LYNCH: Well, we don't have to adopt their arguments either. Let's address ripeness on the merits of ripeness.

MR. BONIFAZ: Well, as we stated at the District Court hearing, Special Operations Troops are already in Iraq laying the groundwork for an invasion. It is clear that this case is ripe. Our soldier plaintiffs should not have to be in a foxhole dodging bullets before they can bring their claims before this court. This is different from Dellums because Dellums did not involve soldier plaintiffs, only Congressional plaintiffs.

Here we have United States soldiers who are about to be put into harms way and they clearly have claims that are ripe. One is a United States Marine based in the Gulf, one has been activated and since sent over since the filing of this case to near northern Iraq, and one has also been activated. So all of these soldier plaintiffs clearly have ripe claims.

JUDGE LYNCH: Suppose the President launches an attack. He reports back to Congress within the period in the October Resolution and Congress' response is a Declaration of War. Has anything unconstitutional happened?

MR. BONIFAZ: Yes, Your Honor, because the President cannot act unless . . .

JUDGE LYNCH: The period up to the point of the Declaration of War was an unconstitutional action by the President even though the Congress authorized what he did?

MR. BONIFAZ: Post-facto?

JUDGE LYNCH: No, I . . . pre . . .

MR. BONIFAZ: Well you just said that if they strike, if the President strikes . . .

JUDGE LYNCH: The President strikes under the October Resolution and reports back to Congress within that forty-eight hour period and the Congress then declares war, has something unconstitutional happened?

MR. BONIFAZ: In between the period of time in which the President went to strike against another nation and Congress declared war, that was unconstitutional. And, furthermore, the framers intended that we would slow down the dogs of war, as Jefferson put it, that we would make this by design a difficult process for the country to get into. Again, the default position is we're not at war. We're not at war. And so in order for us to get into war, Congress must deliberate and vote. And it's not the President to then start a war and then come to Congress and say, now, vote up or down, for or against this war.

JUDGE STAHL: We've had active Air Force engagement in Iraq since 1990, since the cease-fire. My recollection is that we've bombed early-warning devices, the radar, that we run surveillance flights on a daily basis, that we enforce a no-fly zone. Is it your position that all of that also is unconstitutional?

MR. BONIFAZ: No. No, Your Honor, and the distinction is that there is a definition of war that can be achieved here that is different from that.

JUDGE STAHL: A little bit is different than a lot.

MR. BONIFAZ: Well as Judge Green said in Dellum's, that he knows what's before him. He knows that there are three-hundred and fifty thousand (350,000) troops on the border, and in this case two-hundred thousand (200,000) troops and that that is clearly indicating that war is planned. So the facts before this court are what need to be addressed, and the facts before this court involve two-hundred thousand (200,000) troops on the border of Iraq, a clear premeditated planned invasion of that country, a conquering of this country, a public discussion about what's going to happen after the war, occupation of that country for years to come. This is far bigger than limited strikes in a no-fly zone to carry out U.N. mandate prior to that.

JUDGE LYNCH: Can we go back to Judge Cyr's earlier point. I'll defer to Judge Cyr. Go ahead.

JUDGE CYR: Which one?

JUDGE LYNCH: Which of the many points? Alright. The Commander-in-Chief responsibility. Where you have an authorization from Congress to take certain actions and it is possible that there is a war, doesn't the President independently as Commander-in-Chief have some constitutional obligations in this regard and can't he justify what he is doing under the Commander-in-Chief powers?

MR. BONIFAZ: His obligations are as Commander-in-Chief to determine how to fight the war. His obligations are not determined to start the war. That's only Congress' responsibility and it's vested solely in Congress.

JUDGE LYNCH: Alright. Thank you. Mr. Katsas.

MR. KATSAS: Thank you Judge Lynch. May it please The Court, I'm Gregory Katsas appearing for President Bush and Secretary Rumsfeld.

The District Court in this case correctly held that the Plaintiffs challenge to the deployment and possible use of troops by the Commander-in-Chief is a non-justiciable political question, at least absent disagreement by Congress.

JUDGE CYR: As this court has said, resolute conflict.

MR. KATSAS: Absolutely, that's what this court squarely held in Massachusetts vs. Laird upholding a similar war powers challenge to raise a political question. The only difference, Judge Cyr, between this case and Laird is that the Congressional assent is far clearer here where we have an expressed unambiguous approval by Congress of the use of force in contrast to Laird where the court was willing to infer approval from the mere expenditure of money and was willing to do so even in circumstances where that had been an authorization and that authorization had been withdrawn. So we think Laird is controlling and on all fours.

We also have subsequent Supreme Court precedent, I apologize, it's not in our brief. We prepared them quickly. But soon after the Laird case, the Supreme Court decided a case called Gilligan vs. Morgan which is 413 U.S. 1, in which that court similarly held that the control of military force is a political question. And indeed the Supreme Court in that case said it would be harder to imagine a more clear case of a political question than the judgments with respect to the training and control of military force. And the principal difference between the Gilligan case and this one similarly cuts in our favor because the Gilligan case involved the deployment of troops domestically on college campuses. If that raises a political question, then surely the deployment of troops by the Commander-in-Chief in conducting foreign affairs half a world away must as well.

JUDGE STAHL: What do you say about his argument that the use of the phrase "necessary and appropriate" is an unconstitutional delegation of ultimate authority, that it's an open-end delegation?

MR. KATSAS: The question whether the power to declare war on is delegable, Judge Stahl, begs the question, No. 1 of what the declare war power means and No. 2, whether disputes about that question are judicially resolvable. And this court in Massachusetts vs. Laird addressed the merits of the declare war clause to the limited extent of holding very explicitly that that power is not the power to commence war. It's surely not the exclusive power to commence undeclared hostilities. The court said explicitly that the war powers are entrusted to the political branches and more specifically the control over undeclared hostilities is jointly entrusted to the President as Commander-in-Chief and to Congress which of course has the power of the purse.

JUDGE STAHL: Do you see any place where the judiciary would come in play in this scenario? Is there any scenario where we would . . . that you see a role for the judiciary?

MR. KATSAS: It's very hard to imagine, Judge Stahl, because of the system of political checks and balances that this court described in Laird. The President if he wants to engage in undeclared hostilities under our theory, does not have carte-blanche. He needs the Congress to give him the resources. And the Congress if it wants hostilities, obviously doesn't have the executive power to conduct them. So the upshot . . .

JUDGE LYNCH: Yes, but that suggests that the limited remedies under the Constitutional scheme are those available to Congress under the appropriations clause. Bear with me please. Let's assume that a claim were being made here that there was a conflict between Congress and the Executive as to the authorization—that the President was acting plainly in violation of the terms of the authorization. Let's also assume Congress passed a resolution that said, Mr. President, you're violating the resolution. Would you say that courts which normally determine statutory interpretation questions are required to stay out of that?

MR. KATSAS: We would, Judge Lynch, because the political question doctrine is fundamentally not a doctrine about timing but a doctrine about subject matters. This court . . .

JUDGE LYNCH: Well that's one reading of it. There's also another reading of it that it is a doctrine of restraint with about half-a-dozen reasons for it that sometimes prevail, sometimes don't. In Bush vs. Gore, it certainly didn't prevail.

MR. KATSAS: That's true but . . .

JUDGE LYNCH: And the courts have always examined the question of whether something is textually committed to another branch of the government.

MR. KATSAS: Sure, there's always a threshold determination of textual commitment; however, in the Supreme Court's most recent political question decision, which is United States vs. Nixon on impeachment, this issue was joined to some extent because Justice Souter, in a concurring opinion framed the political question doctrine as a prudential doctrine that can be overlooked in cases of impasse citing back to Justice Powell's ripeness analysis in Goldwater.

JUDGE LYNCH: Correct.

MR. KATSAS: The majority in Nixon would have none of that. The majority had no suggestion that the political question holding in that case turned on the absence of impasse. And the Supreme Court in the Gilligan case involving deployment of troops had no suggestion that the political question turned on the absence of impasse. But, Judge Lynch, the most important point for purposes of this case is that the court need not reach the different and possibly more difficult question of what happens when there's impasse.

This court in Laird in the last two sentences of its opinion was very careful to reserve that question. We think it's clearly not presented here because the case of agreement is so clear and so unambiguous. When you read that resolution . . .

JUDGE CYR: But isn't it also true that a week from today, for instance, or tomorrow for that matter, the Congress could pass a bill withdrawing any funding for the military for Iraq, and that would probably put us in a resolute conflict, would it not? between the Executive and the Legislative?

MR. KATSAS: It might well and then a court might be faced with the question that was reserved in Laird and the question that I'm suggesting under both Gilligan and Nixon would be non-justiciable regardless. But that isn't the case where what we have here is Presidential action and a very expressed and unambiguous statement of approval by Congress.

JUDGE LYNCH: It's interesting, if you take the Nixon case and combine it with the Adam Clayton Powell case, there is at least a suggestion that while the form a declaration of war or authorization for war may take is left to the Congress. Once the Congress has determined that form, arguably here the October Resolution, whether there is compliance with the form is a justiciable question.

MR. KATSAS: Under Massachusetts vs. Laird, the court has a threshold determination to make about absence of impasse and that determination you can make, and we think it's dispositive here.

JUDGE LYNCH: And you think that there are ripeness concerns raised both at the level of, is there a actual controversy before the court and at the level of, even if there were, is this a political question for which the fitness and ripeness test is met?

MR. KATSAS: Exactly. There are two components of our ripeness analysis. One is the difficulty of predicting what's going to happen and how hostilities might play out. That, for instance, was the basis on which Judge Lambert found a similar challenge unripe in context of Desert Storm. There is additionally the prudential ripeness concern about the absence of disagreement with the political branches. That concern was expressed by Justice Powell in Goldwater as fundamentally a ripeness concern.

JUDGE LYNCH: Right.

MR. KATSAS: We think it can also be incorporated into a political question analysis to the extent that the day-to-day fluidity, to use Judge Tauro's phrase, will typically be present in situations like this and the impossibility of a court predicting in advance how a situation like this will spin out goes to the absence of judicially manageable standards which is an element of the political question doctrine. Although, frankly, we don't think you need to go beyond textual commitment, which is what Laird found to be enough.

JUDGE STAHL: If we didn't have the war power statute, it didn't exist . . .

MR. KATSAS: Right.

JUDGE STAHL: . . . and the President decided under the circumstances that are facing the country today as he sees them, that a war against Iraq was necessary . . .

MR. KATSAS: Uh-huh.

JUDGE STAHL: . . . does he have the authority under the Constitution to make that determination without Congressional action?

MR. KATSAS: He does, but as a practical matter, he couldn't prosecute the hostilities or the war without resources . . .

JUDGE STAHL: Wait a minute. He's got resources in hand today, he's got a lot of troops overseas now, he doesn't have the War Powers Act, and he hasn't asked for appropriation, as I understand it, yet for the war . . .

MR. KATSAS: Right.

JUDGE STAHL: . . . and he's got them over there and he decides to put them into battle. Historically Congress has never undercut our troops once that happens. Doesn't that make the argument that Congress has the appropriation authority, sort of illusory?

MR. KATSAS: I don't think so. That's the check, that's the system that this court described in Laird. The President has the power of the sword . . .

JUDGE LYNCH: But, I don't think Laird said it was an exclusive power to the exclusion of all other remedies. Let me take Mr. Bonifaz's position into account in this hypothetical. Suppose Congress were to pass a resolution that said, without prior conditions the President can commence a war anywhere anytime he wants. That, at least on the face of it, does seem to be a transfer of Congressional power to the Executive Branch. Would you say, one, that that was non-justiciable and, two, if it was justiciable, would you say it's Constitutional?

MR. KATSAS: As to justiciability, I think I'd need to know more about how the situation plays out if Congress passed that hypothetical declaration and the President made a commitment of troops and Congress did nothing to manifest disagreement, I would say that's clearly non-justiciable under Laird. As to the underlying merits, I will concede that the power to declare war, whatever that may be, is non-delegable. But, again, that just takes us back to the question of what that power is and whether disputes are judicially resolvable. And what this court said in Laird is, that that power is emphatically not, not, the exclusive control over undeclared hostilities.

Judge Stahl, I'd like to just take you back to history and war powers which you mentioned. The War Powers Statute is perhaps the single-best illustration of how breathtakingly radical the Plaintiffs' theory here is. The War Powers Statute is the single-most aggressive assertion by Congress of its control over war powers in American history. Every President since Richard Nixon, who was President when the statute was enacted, has taken the position that the War Powers Act unconstitutionally infringes Executive power.

The War Powers Resolution on its face recognizes that Congress can authorize hostilities without declaring war. So the plaintiffs' position in this case comes down to the proposition that the War Powers Statute is not unconstitutional because it goes too far. Their position must be that the War Powers Statute is unconstitutional because it doesn't go far enough. There is no support for that claim in precedent or in the practices of this country, which brings me to the history point.

There have been something like a hundred to a hundred twenty-five instances of undeclared hostilities in American history. They include the Quasi (phonetic) War with France, which the framing generation fought in the 1790s without a declaration of war. They include the gravest of all American conflicts, the Civil War, and they include the dozen or two, or however many conflicts, every conflict since World War II. There have been only five declarations of war in American history, and the kind of insistent practice and understanding running from the Quasi War with France through to President Clinton's use of hostilities a few years ago in Kosovo, make very clear that there is as little support in practice for the Plaintiffs' theory as there is in legal precedent.

JUDGE CYR: Is the War Powers Act is that the authority for the war against terror?

MR. KATSAS: The Congress passed a resolution authorizing the President or approving Presidential use of force in combating the war against terrorism. I think we could have a similar discussion if there were a challenge to the President's exercise of that power, and I think it would be similarly clear the answer because, No.1, the President supports it and, No. 2, Congress has manifested unambiguous approval.

JUDGE LYNCH: I have a housekeeping question for counsel. Does either side wish to file any further briefs or are you content to rest on the existing briefing to this court? Mr. Bonifaz?

MR. BONIFAZ: We do want to file a supplemental brief, Your Honor.

JUDGE LYNCH: Alright. This court had previously said seven days. Can you live with that? Seven days from today?

MR. BONIFAZ: Fine.

JUDGE LYNCH: Alright. And . . .

MR. KATSAS: We would have been willing to rest, but if there will be briefing, we'd like to have an opportunity . . .

MR. STAHL: In any event, I'd like a 28-J letter on the Gilligan case, I think it was.

MR. KATSAS: We will include the discussion in our brief.

JUDGE LYNCH: You have heard the oral arguments today. I think what I'd prefer is a simultaneous briefing if you don't feel that puts you at a great disadvantage.

MR. KATSAS: No, that's fine Judge Lynch.

JUDGE LYNCH: Then briefs due within seven days of today's hearing. Are there any further questions for counsel? Thank you. It's obviously a case of great moment. It has been extremely well argued by both sides.

(HEARING ENDED)

I, RAYMOND F. CATUOGNO, Registered
Professional Reporter, do hereby certify that the
foregoing testimony prepared from designated
portions of cassettes furnished by the parties
herein, is true and accurate to the best of my
knowledge and belief.

Raymond F. Catuogno
July 22, 2003

To access the plaintiffs' complaint and legal briefs in John Doe I., et al. v. President George W. Bush, et al., *visit* **www.mfso.org.**

Notes

1. 107 P.L. 243; 116 Stat. 1498, Sect. 3(a) (October 16, 2002).
2. Sen. Jacob K. Javits with Don Kellerman, *Who Makes War: The President versus Congress* 13 (New York: William Morrow & Company, Inc., 1973).
3. Louis Fisher, *Presidential War Power* 7 (Lawrence, Kansas: University Press of Kansas, 1995).
4. Id.
5. Id. at 1.
6. Howard Zinn, *A People's History of the United States* 52 (New York: Harper & Row 1980).
7. Id.
8. Id.
9. Id.
10. John Hart Ely, *War and Responsibility: Constitutional Lessons of Vietnam and Its Aftermath* 5 (Princeton, New Jersey: Princeton University Press, 1993).
11. Javits, supra note 2, at 13.
12. Id.
13. Ely, supra note 10, at 5.
14. *Dellums v. Bush,* 752 F. Supp. 1141, 1144 (D.D.C 1990).
15. Fisher, supra note 3, at 7.
16. Ely, supra note 10, at 1.
17. Id. (quoting *The Federalist* No. 69 at 446 (Hamilton) (B. Wright ed. 1961) (emphasis in original)).
18. *Congressional Record,* Vol. 148, S9874, October 3, 2002 (Remarks of Sen. Robert C. Byrd (D-WV), quoting James Madison).
19. Id., quoting Abraham Lincoln.
20. Ely, supra note 10, at 1; Javits, supra note 2, at 14.
21. Zinn, supra note 6, at 466.
22. Id. at 467.
23. Id. at 466.

24. Id. at 467.

25. Id.

26. Id.

27. 88 P.L. 408; 78 Stat. 384 (August 10, 1964).

28. 107 P.L. 243, supra note 1.

29. The resolution the Bush administration presented to Congress did not include the word "imminent." During the rushed congressional debate on the resolution, Senator Richard J. Durbin of Illinois sought to amend the resolution's language to replace the words "the continuing threat posed by Iraq" with "an imminent threat posed by Iraq's weapons of mass destruction." *Congressional Record,* Vol. 148, S10265, October 10, 2002, Amendment No. 4865 (Reading by bill clerk of amendment proposed by Sen. Richard J. Durbin (D-IL)). The administration and its backers in the Senate opposed the amendment, and it was defeated by a vote of 70-30. Id. at S10272. See also President George W. Bush, State of the Union speech, January 28, 2003, available at http://www.whitehouse.gov/news/releases/2003/01/20030128 -19.html: "Some have said we must not act until the threat is imminent."

30. Remarks by President George W. Bush on Iraq, Cincinnati, Ohio, October 7, 2002, available at http://www.white-house.gov/news/releases/2002/10/print/20021007-8.html: "Approving this resolution does not mean that military action is imminent or unavoidable."

31. *Congressional Record,* Vol. 148, H7221, October 8, 2002 (Remarks of Rep. Charles Rangel (D-NY/15)).

32. Id. at H7733, October 9, 2002 (Remarks of Rep. Julia Carson (D-IN/7)).

33. Id. at S10235, October 10, 2002 (Remarks of Sen. Robert C. Byrd (D-WV)).

34. Id. at S10234, October 10, 2002 (Remarks of Sen. Edward M. Kennedy (D-MA)).

35. Id. at S10279, October 10, 2002 (Remarks of Sen. Robert C. Byrd (D-WV)).

36. Id. at S10254, October 10, 2002 (Remarks of Sen. Barbara Boxer (D-CA)).

37. Id.

38. Id. at S10206, October 9, 2002 (Remarks of Sen. Patty Murray (D-WA)).

39. Robert C. Byrd, "Congress Must Resist the Rush to War," New York Times, October 10, 2002.

40. James Kuhnhenn, "Congress feels Bush's force on Iraq," Philadelphia Inquirer, October 7, 2002.

41. Congressional Record, Vol. 148, S10165, October 9, 2002 (Remarks of Sen. Robert C. Byrd (D-WV)).

42. Id. at H7780, October 10, 2002 (Remarks of Rep. Richard K. Armey (R-TX/26)).

43. Id. at H7732, October 9, 2002 (Remarks of Rep. Wally Herger (R-CA/2)).

44. Id. at S10150, October 9, 2002 (Remarks of Sen. Kay Bailey Hutchison (R-TX)).

45. Id. at H7722, October 9, 2002 (Remarks of William Delahunt (D-MA/10)).

46. Id., citing Dana Priest, "Analysts Discount Attack by Iraq," Washington Post, October 9, 2002.

47. Id., citing Warren P. Strobel, Jonathan S. Landay and John Walcott, "Dissent Over Going to War Grows Among U.S. Government Officials," Miami Herald, October 8, 2002.

48. Id.

49. Id. at H7723.

50. Id. at S10152, October 9, 2002 (Remarks of Sen. Patrick Leahy (D-VT)).

51. Id. at S10154.

52. Id. at H7396, October 9, 2002 (Remarks of Rep. Sheila Jackson-Lee (D-TX/18)).

53. Id. at H7396-7397.

54. Id. at H7397.

55. Id. at H7276, October 8, 2002 (Remarks of Rep. Jim McDermott (D-WA/7)).

56. Id.

57. Id.

58. Id.

59. Id. at S10238, October 10, 2002 (Remarks of Sen. Robert C. Byrd (D-WV)).

60. Id.

61. Id. at S10247-10248.

62. Id. at S10248.

63. Id. at S10275.

64. Id. at S10249, October 10, 2002 (Remarks of Sen. Joseph R. Biden (D-DE)).

65. Id.

66. Id. at S10290.

67. Id. at H7389, October 9, 2002 (Remarks of Rep. Carolyn B. Maloney (D-NY/14)).

68. Id. at S10293, October 10, 2002 (Remarks of Sen. Joseph R. Biden (D-DE)).

69. Id.

70. Id. at S10296.

71. Id.

72. Id. at S10174, October 9, 2002 (Remarks of Sen. John F. Kerry (D-MA)).

73. Id.

74. Id. at S10175.

75. Seymour M. Hersh, "Who Lied To Whom?", *The New Yorker*, March 31, 2003, 42.

76. Id.

77. Id. at 43.

78. President George W. Bush, Remarks by the President to the Press Pool, December 31, 2002, available at http://www.state.gov/p/eap/rls/rm/2002/16627.htm

79. *Marbury v. Madison,* 5 U.S. (1 Cranch) 137, 177 (1803).

80. *Little v. Barreme,* 6 U.S. (2 Cranch) 170, 179 (1804).

81. *United States v. Brown,* 12 U.S. (8 Cranch) 110, 125-27 (1814).

82. *Fleming v. Page,* 50 U.S. (9 How.) 603, 615, 618 (1850).

83. *Youngstown Sheet & Tube Co. v. Sawyer,* 343 U.S. 579 (1952).

84. Fisher, supra note 3, at 101; *Youngstown* at 583.

85. *Youngstown* at 583.

86. Id.

87. Id.

88. Id.

89. Id.

90. Fisher, supra note 3, at 101; *Youngstown* at 584.

91. Fisher at 101, citing "U.S. Argues President Is Above Courts," *New York Times,* April 25, 1952, A1.

92. Id., quoting Public Papers of the Presidents, 1952, 273.

93. Id. at 102, quoting Public Papers of the Presidents, 1952, 273.

94. Id., quoting *Youngstown Sheet & Tube Co. v. Sawyer,* 103 F. Supp. 569, 577 (D.D.C. 1952).

95. *Youngstown,* 343 U.S. at 587.

96. Id. at 629-630 (Douglas, J., concurring).

97. Id. at 632.

98. Id. at 633.

99. Id. at 655, (Jackson, J., concurring).

100. Leon Friedman and Burt Neuborne, *Unquestioning Obedience to the President: The ACLU Case Against the Legality of the War in Vietnam* 25 (New York: W.W. Norton & Company, Inc., 1972).

101. Id.

102. Fisher, supra note 3, at 84.

103. Id. at 86-87.

104. Id. at 86.

105. *United States v. Bolton,* 192 F.2d 805, 806 (2d Cir. 1951).

106. Id.

107. Friedman and Neuborne, supra note 100, at 25.

108. *United States v. Mitchell,* 246 F. Supp. 874, 897 (D. Conn. 1965).

109. Id. at 898.

110. Id.

111. Id.

112. Id.

113. Id.

114. Id. at 899.

115. *United States v. Mitchell,* 369 F.2d 323, 324 (2d Cir. 1966).

116. *Baker v. Carr,* 369 U.S. 186 (1962).

117. *Kidd v. McCanless,* 200 Tenn. 273, 282 (1956).

118. *Baker* at 237.

119. *Reynolds v. Sims,* 377 U.S. 533, 566 (1964).

120. *Luftig v. McNamara,* 373 F.2d 664 (D.C. Cir. 1967).

121. Id. at 665.

122. Id.

123. Id. at 655-666.

124. *Mora v. McNamara,* 389 U.S. 934 (1967).

125. Id., (Stewart, J. and Douglas, J., dissenting).

126. Id.

127. Id. at 935.

128. Friedman and Neuborne, supra note 100, at 29.

129. *United States v. Holmes,* 391 U.S. 936, 949 (1968) (Douglas, J., dissenting).

130. Friedman and Neuborne, supra note 100, at 30.

131. Id.

132. Id.

133. Zinn, supra note 6, at 474.

134. Friedman and Neuborne, supra note 100, at 30.

135. Id.

136. Id.

137. Id.

138. Id. at 35.

139. Id. at 38.

140. Id.

141. Id. at 39.

142. *Orlando v. Laird,* 443 F. 2d 1039, 1040 (2d Cir. 1971, quoting *Orlando v. Laird,* 317 F. Supp. 1013, 1019) (E.D.N.Y. 1970).

143. Id. at 1042.

144. Id.

145. Id.

146. *DaCosta v. Laird,* 448 F.2d 1368, 1369 (2d Cir. 1971).

147. *Mottola v. Nixon,* 318 F. Supp. 538, 540 (N.D. Cal. 1970).

148. Id. at 547, n.12.

149. Id. at 550.

150. Id. at 553-554.

151. Id. at 553.

152. *Mottola v. Nixon,* 464 F.2d 178 (9th Cir. 1972).

153. *Mitchell v. Laird,* 488 F. 2d 611, 615 (D.C. Cir. 1973).

154. Id.

155. Id. at 616.

156. Ely, supra note 10, at 34.

157. *Holtzman v. Richardson,* 361 F. Supp. 544, 547 (E.D.N.Y. 1973).

158. Zinn, supra note 6, at 474; Christopher Hitchens, *The Trial of Henry Kissinger* 35 (London/New York: Verso, 2001).

159. *Holtzman v. Schelsinger,* 484 F.2d 1307, 1308 (2d Cir. 1973).

160. Id.

161. Id.

162. Id.

163. Id.

164. Ely, supra note 10, at 34.

165. *Holtzman v. Schlesinger,* 414 U.S. 1316, 1317 (1973).

166. *Holtzman v. Schlesinger,* 361 F. Supp. 553, 565.

167. *Holtzman v. Schlesinger,* 414 U.S. 1320.

168. Id.

169. *Schlesinger v. Holtzman,* 414 U.S. 1321 (1973).

170. Id.

171. Id. at 1323 (Douglas, J. dissenting).

172. Id. at 1324, 1326.

173. Id. at 1326.

174. *Holtzman v. Schlesinger,* 484 F.2d 1307, 1311, 1313-1314 (2d Cir. 1973).

175. Id. at 1318 (Oakes, J., dissenting).

176. Id.

177. *Drinan v. Nixon,* 364 F. Supp. 854, 858 (D. Mass. 1973).

178. Memorandum In Support of Defendants' Motion to Dismiss And In Opposition To Plaintiffs' Motion for Preliminary Injunction (Defendants' Opposition Memorandum), 4, filed in the U.S. District Court for the District of Massachusetts in Doe v. Bush (on file with the author).

179. "Project Iraq," ABC-*Nightline,* April 23, 2003, available at http://abcnews.go.com/Sections/Nightline/

180. *Dellums v. Bush,* 752 F. Supp. 1141 (D.D.C. 1990).

181. Id. at 1146.

182. Id. at 1151.

183. Plaintiffs' Reply Brief, 9, filed in the U.S. District Court for the District of Massachusetts in *Doe v. Bush* (on file with the author and available at www.mfso.org).

184. *Conyers v. Reagan,* 578 F. Supp. 324 (D.D.C. 1984).

185. Plaintiffs' Reply Brief at 11.

186. Thomas E. Ricks, "U.S. troops in Iraq: War's initial ground phase under way," *Washington Post,* February 13, 2003, A1.

187. Id.

188. Id.

189. Id.

190. Defendants' Opposition Memorandum, 4.

191. *Doe v. Bush,* Memorandum and Order, Civil Action No. 03-10284-JLT, U.S. District Judge Joseph L. Tauro, U.S. District Court, District of Massachusetts, February 24, 2003 (on file with the author).

192. Id. at 2.

193. Id.

194. Notes of April 2003 interview with Derege B. Demissie, attorney for Diland Herbert.

195. *Campbell v. Clinton,* 203 F.3d 19, 20 (D.C. Cir. 2000).

196. Id.

197. Id. at 37 (Tatel, J., concurring).

198. 93 P.L. 148; 87 Stat. 555 (November 7, 1973).

199. Brief Submitted On Behalf of 74 Concerned Law Professors As Amici Curiae Supporting The Request of Appellants for Reversal, 2, filed before the U.S. Court of Appeals for the First Circuit in *Doe v. Bush* (on file with the author and available at www.mfso.org).

200. Id.

201. *Doe v. Bush,* 323 F.3d 133, 143 (1st Cir., March 13, 2003).

202. *Clinton v. City of New York,* 524 U.S. 417 (1998).

203. *Doe v. Bush,* 323 F.3d at 142.

204. Id.

205. Id.

206. Id., quoting *Massachusetts v. Laird,* 451 F.2d 26, 31-32 (1st Cir. 1971) (emphasis omitted).

207. 107 P.L. 243, 116 Stat. 1498, 1501, Sect. 3(a)(2).

208. *Doe v. Bush,* 323 F.3d at 139.

209. Id.

210. Id.

211. "Bush: Monday is 'a moment of truth' on Iraq," CNN.com, March 17, 2003, www.cnn.com.

212. *Doe v. Bush,* 323 F.3d at 141.

213. Plaintiffs/Appellants' Petition for Rehearing on an Emergency Basis, 4, filed before the U.S. Court of Appeals for the First Circuit in *Doe v. Bush* (on file with the author and available at www.mfso.org).

214. Id.

215. *Doe v. Bush*, 322 F.3d 109, 110 (1st Cir., March 18, 2003).

216. Id, quoting *Massachusetts v. Laird*, 451 F.2d at 34.

217. Barton Gellman, "Frustrated, U.S. Arms Team to Leave Iraq: Task Force Unable to Find Any Weapons," *Washington Post*, May 11, 2003, A1.

218. Id.

219. Id.

220. Id.

221. Raymond Whitaker, "Revealed: How the Road to War was Paved with Lies: Intelligence agencies accuse Bush and Blair of distorting and fabricating evidence in rush to war," *The Independent*, April 27, 2003, www.independent.co.uk.

222. Id.

223. President George W. Bush, State of the Union speech, January 28, 2003, available at http://www.whitehouse.gov/news/releases/2003/01/20030128-19.html

224. Id.

225. Id.

226. "The War Behind Closed Doors: Excerpts from 1992 Draft 'Defense Planning Guidance,'" PBS-*Frontline*, February 20, 2003, available at http://www.pbs.org/wgbh/pages/frontline/shows/iraq/etc/wolf.html

227. Id.

228. Id.

229. Barton Gellman, "Keeping the U.S. First: Pentagon Would Preclude a Rival Superpower," *Washington Post*, March 11, 1992, A1.

230. Id.

231. "The War Behind Closed Doors," PBS-*Frontline*, Feb-

ruary 20, 2003, transcript at 6, available at http://www.pbs.org/wgbh/pages/frontline/shows/iraq/etc/tapes.html

232. Id. at 6-7.

233. Patrick E. Tyler, "Pentagon Drops Goal of Blocking New Superpowers," *New York Times,* May 24, 1992, A1.

234. William Rivers Pitt, "Of Gods and Mortals and Empire," www.truthout.org, February 21, 2003.

235. Id.

236. "The Plan: Were Neo-Conservatives' 1998 Memos a Blueprint for Iraq War?" ABCNEWS.com, March 10, 2003, www.abcnews.com.

237. Id.

238. "Rebuilding America's Defenses: Strategy, Forces and Resources for a New Century," Project for the New American Century, September 2000, (2000 PNAC report) available at http://www.newamericancentury.org/publicationsreports.htm

239. Id. at ii.

240. Id. at iv.

241. Neil MacKay, "Bush Planned Iraq 'Regime Change' Before Becoming President," *The Sunday Herald* (Scotland), September 15, 2002, available at http://www.sundayherald.com/27735.

242. Id.

243. Id.

244. 2000 PNAC report at 4.

245. Id. at 50.

246. Id. at 50.

247. Id. at 51.

248. "The Plan," ABCNEWS-*Nightline* Transcript, March 5, 2003, 3, www.transcripts.net.

249. Id.

250. "The War Behind Closed Doors," PBS-*Frontline,* February 20, 2003, available at http://www.pbs.org/wgbh/pages/frontline/shows/iraq/etc/cron.html

251. Nicholas Lemann, "The Next World Order: The Bush Administration may have a brand-new doctrine of power," *The New Yorker,* April 1, 2002.

252. "The War Behind Closed Doors," PBS-*Frontline,* February 20, 2003, available at http://www.pbs.org/wgbh/pages/frontline/shows/iraq/etc/cron.html

253. President George W. Bush, "Remarks by the President at 2002 Graduation Exercise of the United States Military Academy, West Point, New York," June 1, 2002, available at http://www.white house.gov/news/releases/2002/06/20020601-3.html

254. Thomas E. Ricks and Vernon Loeb, "Bush Developing Military Policy Of Striking First," *Washington Post,* June 10, 2002, A1.

255. "The National Security Strategy of the United States of America," The White House, September 2002, available at http://www.whitehouse.gov/nsc/nss.html

256. "The War Behind Closed Doors," PBS-*Frontline,* February 20, 2003, available at http://www.pbs.org/wgbh/pages/frontline/shows/iraq/themes/1992.html

257. Seymour M. Hersh, "Selective Intelligence," *The New Yorker,* May 12, 2003, 44.

258. Id.

259. Id.

260. Id.

261. Id. at 48.

262. Id. at 51.

263. Id.

264. Id.

265. Mike Allen and Barton Gellman, "Preemptive Strikes Part of U.S. Strategic Doctrine," *Washington Post,* December 11, 2002, A1.

266. Arthur Schlesinger Jr., "Today, It Is We Americans Who Live in Infamy," *Los Angeles Times,* March 23, 2003.

267. Id.

268. Id.

Acknowledgments

I am grateful to the many people who made this book possible and who have provided support and advice along the way.

It was an honor to have represented a coalition of courageous individuals who served as plaintiffs in *John Doe I, et al. v. President George W. Bush, et al.* Standing at the front were the two United States soldiers and one United States Marine courageously serving as the lead plaintiffs in this case (with their identities protected to prevent retaliation by the U.S. military). They took the most risk in fighting for the United States Constitution.

Standing with them were brave parents of members of the U.S. armed forces: Nancy Lessin and Charley Richardson, Jeffrey McKenzie, Susan E. Schumann, Jerrye Barre, Alice Copeland Brown, James Stephen Cleghorn, Julian and Rose Delgaudio, Laura Johnson Manis, Deborah Regal, Sally Wright, Shirley H. Young, and two parents whose identities remain protected. These plaintiffs were joined by twelve members of the United States Congress who followed their oath of office and challenged a United States president for his march toward an illegal and unconstitutional war. Led by Representatives John Conyers, Jr. and Dennis Kucinich, the other congressional plaintiffs included: Rep. Jesse Jackson, Jr.,

Rep. Sheila Jackson Lee, Rep. Jim McDermott, Rep. José E. Serrano, Rep. Danny K. Davis, Rep. Maurice D. Hinchey, Rep. Carolyn Kilpatrick, Rep. Pete Stark, Rep. Diane Watson, and Rep. Lynn C. Woolsey.

I am fortunate to have worked with an incredible legal team. I could not have done this case without my law partner and father, Cristóbal Bonifaz, whose passion and dedication to the cause of justice knows no bounds. Further, I am grateful to our other co-counsel: Professor Margaret Burnham of Northeastern University School of Law; and Max Stern and Jonathan Shapiro of Stern Shapiro Weissberg & Garin. Our legal team received crucial assistance from several students at Harvard Law School. I am especially grateful to Clifford Ginn, who, in his third year at Harvard Law School, played a critical role, devoting enormous energy to this case under tight time constraints and producing outstanding work throughout the process. I am also appreciative of the contributions from law students Thom Cmar, George Farah, Andrew Fishkoff, Michael Gottlieb, and Amanda Straub, and from attorney Ross Scott in this litigation. There are others in the legal community who provided invaluable help with this case and they know who they are. Thank you.

When this case reached the U.S. Court of Appeals for the First Circuit in Boston on an expedited basis, a coalition of seventy-four law professors from around the country filed an important friend-of-the-court brief in support of our legal arguments. Professor Marie Ashe of Suffolk University School of Law served as the principal author of that brief. I am grateful to her and to Professor Michael Avery of Suffolk University School of Law for coordinating all of the brief's signatories.

I owe special thanks to John Moyers, Ellen Miller, and Nick Penniman of TomPaine.com for their support and their early willingness to publish an op-ed that served as a prelude to the filing of our lawsuit. I am also appreciative of Andy Morris, Carol Klenfner, and Justin Kazmark for their help. I am grateful to Conrad Martin and the Fund for Constitutional Government in Washington, D.C., and to Ian Thorne Simmons for their assistance with legal expenses connected to this case, and I thank the Traprock Peace Center in Deerfield, Massachusetts for its support.

My special thanks goes to Burton Wides in Representative Conyers' office for his critical support and to Jaron Bourke and Sapna Chhatpar in Representative Kucinich's office, and Frank Watkins in Representative Jackson's office for their assistance with this case. I thank Steve Cobble for his strategic advice during the initiation of this case.

I was privileged to have been able to work closely during this litigation with plaintiffs Nancy Lessin and Charley Richardson, the co-founders, with plaintiff Jeffrey McKenzie, of Military Families Speak Out (www.mfso.org), an organization of people who oppose the war in Iraq and who have family members and loved ones in the military. Nancy and Charley were tireless in their dedication to this case, and their eloquence and passion always moved me. I am thankful to Joseph Gerson of the American Friends Service Committee for the New England Region for serving as my link to Nancy and Charley.

A special debt of gratitude is owed to my friend Steven Lewis for his catalytic role in making this case happen and for sharing the vision that it had to be done.

As this case came to a close in March 2003, my friend Steven Donziger encouraged me to begin writing this book. I thank him for believing in this project and for all of his crucial support.

I have received invaluable assistance from many people who have reviewed drafts of this book, including: Deirdre Bonifaz, Cristóbal Bonifaz, Lissa Pierce, Steven Lewis, Jason Adkins, Hilary Binda, Steven Donziger, Clifford Ginn, Gregory Luke, and Burton Wides. Thank you for your time and your critical help. I am appreciative of Derege B. Demissie's assistance.

I owe special thanks to Carl Bromley and my publisher Nation Books, and to my agent Liza Dawson. I also owe special thanks to Marnie Mueller for introducing me to Liza.

I thank Beau Friedlander and Trevor Bundy for their key assistance.

Finally, I thank the people in my life for their love and support: Deirdre, Cristóbal, and Margarita Bonifaz, and Lissa Pierce.

John C. Bonifaz is an attorney in Boston, Massachusetts, with the Law Offices of Cristóbal Bonifaz. Mr. Bonifaz is also the founder and executive director of the National Voting Rights Institute, a prominent legal center in the campaign finance reform field. Mr. Bonifaz is a 1999 recipient of a MacArthur Foundation Fellowship. He is a 1992 graduate of Harvard Law School and a 1987 graduate of Brown University.

Mr. Bonifaz served as lead counsel for the plaintiffs in *John Doe I et al. v. President George W. Bush, et al.*

Congressman John Conyers, Jr. represents the Fourteenth Congressional District of Michigan. First elected in 1964, Mr. Conyers was re-elected in November 2002 to his nineteenth term and is the second most senior member of the United States House of Representatives. Mr. Conyers leads the Democratic side of the House Committee on the Judiciary. He was a member of the House Judiciary Committee in its 1974 hearings on the Watergate impeachment scandal. Congressman Conyers is considered the Dean of the Congressional Black Caucus.

Mr. Conyers served as a lead congressional plaintiff in *John Doe I et al. v. President George W. Bush, et al.*